Good walk
Good pub
South Lakes

footstep
PUBLISHING LTD

Every effort has been made to ensure that the information in this publication is accurate. The publisher accepts no responsibility whatsoever for any injury, loss or inconvenience incurred by any person or persons whilst using this book.

Published by
Footstep Publishing Ltd
Rose Cottage, Priest Hutton, Carnforth LA6 1JP
www.footstep-publishing.com

ISBN 13: 978-0-9553727-0-4
ISBN 10: 0-9553727-0-4

Cover illustration and book design by Gary Lawson (www.g1creative.co.uk)
Photography by Meg Brady, Keith Brady and Geoff Harris

Printed in England

Good walk
Good pub
South Lakes

good

20 CIRCULAR WALKS WITH A PUB IN THE MIDDLE

Contents

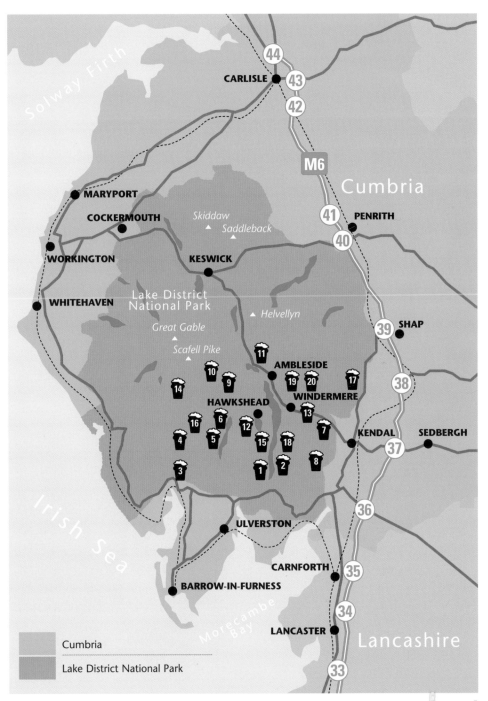

Introduction

This book is born out of frustration. It's the frustration of having shelves sagging under the weight of years of accumulated walking guides, many of them excellent publications, yet all of them flawed in one key area. They fail to address the vital question at the very core of what it is to be a human being, the question that daily hangs at the back of conscious thought from the moment of waking: "Where am I going to get my lunch?"

The subject of 'refreshments' is covered of course, but the pubs mentioned (sometimes cafés) are invariably at the beginning/end of the walk. What's the good of that? If I want to include a pub lunch in my day's outing it means that I have to rush along the route, repeatedly checking the time and prodding tardy companions if we are to stand any chance of reaching our goal before the chef hangs up his hat at two o'clock. It is true that with the relaxation of licensing laws, pubs tend to stay open for much longer during the day but even so, most kitchens generally shut up shop at around two.

What about starting the walk earlier? Yes, it's possible, but for any walk in excess of four hours it means knotting the boot-laces and hauling on the rucksack by nine o'clock and, if you have any distance to travel before walking, then leaving the house has to be a disciplined affair – more like a day at work really. This is not what we are after on a day off, well-earned or otherwise.

Perfect days rarely happen by themselves, they need a little planning. This is where *Good Walk Good Pub* comes in. What could be better than an energising walk with friends or family through idyllic landscapes,

a good lunch made with local produce, eaten in comfortable surroundings and all washed down with a hop-scented glass from the nearby brewery? Follow this with a gentle return trip and you have the recipe for a perfect day for both mind and body – **an uplifting blend of exercise and indulgence**.

All the pubs chosen for this guide were selected on the basis of quality – food, beer, service and surroundings. At the time of the visits, none of the establishments involved were aware that we were compiling this guide and there has been no financial involvement from either pubs or breweries. This book is completely impartial and reflects only the views of the author.

Real ale is a feature common to all the pubs visited, and the Lake District is particularly well served by local breweries with no less than twenty producing traditional beers (includes Dent Brewery, which is slightly outside our area, but well worth including). Only one, Jennings Brewery, could be termed a regional brewer and, not surprisingly, this is the oldest, founded in 1828. All the others are much smaller and were started by enthusiasts following the birth of the Campaign for Real Ale (CAMRA). None is older than twenty years. Without exception, all twenty of them make delicious beers.

Since the outbreak of foot and mouth disease in 2001, and the destruction of livestock that followed, upland farming can now only be described as "challenging" as a way of making a living. Many farmers have, however, risen to the challenge and

Cumbrian Duck Sausage Salad -
The Mason's Arms, Strawberry Bank

Good walk, Good pub

the North West of England now has some exceptional producers of meats, cheese and other foods, many of them supplying direct to the public through farm shops and farmers' markets and many, of course, to the pubs in our guide. The White Hart at Bouth (Walk 1) does a sell-out Steak & Guinness Pie made with beef from Abbotts Reading Farm, barely two miles from the pub, beyond the old gunpowder works; or why not try the Kentmere Lamb Hotpot at the Eagle & Child in Staveley, at the foot of the Kentmere valley (Walk 17).

The process of putting together the routes for these walks began, naturally enough, with the pub. Some of the walks are re-workings of old favourites, others are more 'original' as routes and follow less frequently used paths. Not all the footpaths used are necessarily shown by the Ordnance Survey as rights of way. There have been significant changes in access to the countryside in recent years and 'permissive' paths through areas owned by the Forestry Commission and through nature reserves are regular features of these walks.

Without doubt, the most difficult decision in designing the routes was where to begin - pubs are generally situated in areas of population. Without the locals to keep them going, many pubs would not survive the quiet months of winter. If we start the walk about two or three hours away on foot, this is very often not in an area of population. The overriding concern has been to find an appropriate place to park the car at the start. This has been done for all the walks. If there was not sufficient room for several cars, then we had to think of somewhere else to start. We even abandoned a wonderful walk from

Kentmere village over the Garburn Pass to Troutbeck when, on re-visiting to check the walk, it became obvious that there was nowhere to reasonably leave a car in the village, with its single track access, if one arrived after 9.30 am and the six or so places had already been taken for the day.

The one dilemma in deciding where to start has been that, though we truly want to encourage the use of public transport as much as possible, some starts are less than easy if you want to arrive by bus. Where this is the case, some adjustments will need to be made when using the route. Details of public transport services can be found on the websites listed on page 13.

All the walks are designed to be more challenging in the first half, before the pub. As often as not, the pub is to be found nearer to two thirds of the way round, rather than in the middle, and this is deliberate. You should arrive at the pub with the smug self-congratulating air of someone who knows that he's earned his lunch. You can also be fairly confident that the steepest of climbs and the bulk of the legwork are behind you.

Meg

How to use this book

This book contains 20 walks with all routes including a pub on the way. The pubs have been chosen for the quality of their food, beer and welcome. They are all worth the effort of getting there.

Each walk includes a map based on the Ordnance Survey 1:25000 series and, with the exception of Walks 3, 4, 6, 12, 14, and 17, they are printed at the correct scale. You should always, however, make sure that you carry the relevant OS map covering the wider area. You never know when you might stray from your intended path. The routes used in this book are covered by OS Explorer OL6 & OL7 maps.

The times given should be used as a rough guide and refer to walking time only. Most of the walks take little more than 2 hours before the pub, and most are shorter on the return journey. You should allow at least an hour at the pub.

When planning your walk, always look carefully at pub opening times, particularly on weekdays. It is no longer the case that pubs open for regular and predictable times. Many now stay open much later at the weekends and may take a day off in the week to compensate. If you are trying to impress your boss, girlfriend, or mother-in-law, phone first to check before walking midweek.

The walks are graded in terms of physical difficulty and this is shown on the contents page and repeated in the fact page at the beginning of each walk description.

The grading is as follows:

Easy:
not particularly far and with only minor ascents and descents.

Moderate:
does include some ascents and descents though not very strenuous.

Strenuous:
might include more strenuous ascents and descents, some distance and possibly some rough terrain.

Comfortable lightweight boots are probably the best footwear for all the walks in this guide. They give support to the ankle and can help to minimise twists and sprains. A good rubber sole with plenty of grip also helps to improve confidence in where to step - particularly important in descents - and adds to the general enjoyment in walking. It is always advisable to take waterproof clothing, whatever the weather when you set out. Conditions on the Lake District fells can change remarkably quickly and you should be prepared for the worst. Make sure you take plenty of water, and in summer especially, I would also recommend some insect repellant and sun block.

What to take

Water
Mobile phone
OS Map e.g Explorer OL6 & OL7
Compass
First Aid kit

Walking pole (if necessary)
Water proofs
Walking boots
Money
Thick socks

Some of the footpaths in the Lake District are very old and represent thousands of years of people on the move. To follow in the footsteps of generations of Mesolithic hunters, traders in stone tools (see Walk 10), conquering armies, beleaguered natives, cattle drovers, miners, monks and packhorse drivers is a fairly humbling experience and we should guard this heritage with care. The impact of mass tourism on the area has had considerable consequences in terms of erosion of footpaths and our modern needs for comfort and safety, in the form of heavy boots and walking poles, may possibly be adding to the problem. Always keep to the path and try to avoid widening it by wandering.

On the subject of wandering, we have noticed during our months of tireless research on this project that there is a much greater risk of straying from the intended route in the moments immediately after leaving the pub. There are reasons for this beyond the obvious ones. You may be waiting for companions to lace up, zip up etc. and the party divides. The last person out is invariably the one with the book, matters of deep philosophical importance are being discussed and there is a general feeling of bonhomie. Having once re-gained the route it is a good idea to look two or three steps ahead in the walk instructions to avoid missing a critical point of navigation.

It goes without saying that it is best not to overdo things in the pub, always leave plenty of time during daylight to get back and stay within the legal limits if you are the driver. Neither beer nor Cumberland sausages are performance-enhancing foods and legs can seem surprisingly reluctant to work with enthusiasm on the homeward journey.

Transport

Although all our walks begin with a place to park the car, we also actively encourage the use of public transport. During the summer months, the Lake District can become congested with holidaymakers' cars and caravans, causing pollution and damage to the environment. However, the Lake District has excellent public transport links that take you, your bikes and your equipment, all over the county, not only to the towns but to the remote villages and hamlets as well.

Allowing someone else to do the driving has many advantages. As all our walks feature a fantastic pub along the way, not having the responsibility of driving you and your fellow walkers home can free you to enjoy more of Cumbria's finest local ale! We do, however, stress that too much beer is more of a hindrance than help where the final stretch of the walk is concerned.

Another advantage is that you can really enjoy the beautiful Lake District scenery from the comfort of the train, a bus or a boat. Or, if you are anything like my father and I, the journey back home after a long day out in the fresh air is the best time to have a short nap. How better to enjoy 40 winks than have someone else do the driving and navigating!

Use the numbers or websites on the page opposite to find out travel information for coach, bus, train and boat. You could also visit the Lake District National Park Authority website **www.lake-district.gov.uk**, where you can find fares and timetables for public transport links as well as ideas for visitor attractions around the Lakes so you can enjoy a car-free day and help to reduce the adverse impact of motor traffic on the environment.

Getting around the Lakes

COACH/BUS

Traveline provide information by phone or the Internet on all their coach/bus services. Browse online to view timetables for all the services below, just by entering the service number. They also provide a Journey Planner.

> Traveline - 0870 608 2608

> www.traveline.org.uk

555 Lakeslink
599 Windermere Open Top Bus
Borrowdale Rambler (79)
Caldbeck Rambler (73/73A)
Coniston Rambler (505)
Ennerdale Rambler (263)
Haweswater Rambler (111)
Honister Rambler (77/77A)
Kentmere Rambler (519)
Kirkstone Rambler (517)
Langdale Rambler (516)
Patterdale Bus
Tarn Hows Tourer (National Trust)
Ulswater Connexion
Watendlath Wanderer (National Trust)

MOUNTAIN GOAT

The **Mountain Goat** company offers tours, private hire and shuttle services around the Lakes, teaming you up with ferry services or carrying you and your bikes or boots off the beaten track.

015394 45161 **(Windermere)** or 017687 73962 **(Keswick)**
(Plus **Windermere/Bowness** Shuttle, Cross Lakes Shuttle)

> www.mountain-goat.com

> enquiries@mountain-goat.com

FERRY

Windermere and Coniston run foot passenger ferries or steamer services that will take you across the lake. **Windermere Car Ferry** operates regular shuttle services throughout the year between Bowness-on-Windermere and Far Sawrey. These crossings may be cancelled in bad weather, so for more information and confirmation of crossing times, telephone the number below.

> Ferry Hotline - 0860 813 427

> Windermere Lake Cruises – 015394 31188

GETTING TO AND FROM THE LAKES

The nearest international airport is **Manchester Airport**. Trains run daily from the airport and stop at **Lancaster, Carnforth, Oxenholme (Lake District)** and **Penrith**. From **Oxenholme** you can get the train across to **Kendal** and **Windermere**, and from **Lancaster** the trains run to **Arnside, Grange-over-Sands, Ulverston** and **Barrow** along the Furness Line.

> National Rail Enquiries – 08457 48 49 50

> www.nationalrail.co.uk

National Express Rapide services run from London (Victoria) to Kendal, Ulverston, Ambleside, Barrow and Windermere.

> National Express – 08705 80 80 80

> www.GoByCoach.com

White Hart
Bouth

Grid reference SD 328 857

Licensee	Nigel and Peter Barton
Brewery	Free House
Tel	01229 861229
Fax	✗
Website	www.bed-and-breakfast-cumbria.co.uk
Email	nigelwhitehart@aol.com
Description	Traditional village pub, with low ceilings and open fires.
Opening Hours	Mon – Tues 6pm – 11pm, Wed – Fri 12pm – 2pm 6pm –11pm
	Sat 12pm 11pm, Sun 12pm – 10.30pm
Food Serving Times	12am – 2pm 6pm – 8.45pm (Closed Mon and Tues lunchtimes)
Child Friendly	Children's Menu (under 12s only)
Disabled Access/Facilities	✓
Dog Friendly	✗
Beer Garden	✓
Log Fire/Stove	✓
Storage area	✓
Smoking in Bar	No Smoking
Food	Freshly cooked using local ingredients. Locally reared beef, pork
	and lamb from Abbots Reading Farm. Scottish Salmon Fillet £8.95,
	Homemade Lamb & Apricot Pie £6.95
Beer (price per pint)	Black Sheep £2.10, Yates Bitter £2.10,
	Jennings Cumberland Ale £2.10
Guest Beers (price per pint)	Timothy Taylor Landlord £2.40, Copper Dragon Pippin £2.35,
	Highgate Dark Mild £2.10
Wine	Rioja £14, Beaujolais Village £12
Extras	Accommodation available

Hare & Hounds
Bowland Bridge

Grid reference SD 417 895

Licensee	Adrian Parr
Brewery	Jennings
Tel	015395 68333
Fax	015395 68777
Website	X
Email	X
Description	Lovely village setting, flagstone floors and friendly service
Opening Hours – Summer	(Mar to Nov) Mon – Fri 11am – 3 pm 5.30pm – 11pm
	Sat 11am – 11pm Sun 12pm – 11pm
Opening Hours – Winter	(Nov to Mar) Same as above, but closed Tuesdays.
Serving Times	Mon – Fri 12pm – 2pm 5.30 pm – 9pm
	Sat – Sun 12pm – 2.30pm 5.30pm – 9pm
	(Sat/Sun 5.45pm in Winter)
Child Friendly	Children's menu and outdoor play area
Disabled Access	X
Dog Friendly	X
Beer Garden/Outdoor Seating	✓
Log Fire/Stove	✓
Storage area	✓
Smoking in Bar	Separate smoking/non-smoking areas
Food	Well known for fresh seafood, local fell-bred meat and organic meat.
	Grilled Seabass £13.95, Local Lamb Shank £12.50
Beer (price per pint)	Hare Beer £2.10, Jennings Bitter £2.10, Cumberland Ale £2.20
Guest Beers	Seasonally
Wine	Choice of 40 wines from £11.50/bottle
Extras	Hare Beer is specially brewed for the Hare & Hounds Inn

Old King's Head
Broughton-In-Furness

Grid reference SD 211 875

Licensee	Russell & Damien Clarke
Brewery	Free House
Tel	01229 716 293
Fax	01229 715 165
Email	enquiries@oldkingshead.co.uk
Web	www.oldkingshead.co.uk
Description	One of the oldest buildings in Broughton, this family run inn offers friendly service and fantastic food.
Opening Hours	11am - 11pm
Food Serving Times	Mon – Sat 12 – 2pm 6pm – closing Sun 12 - 8pm
Child Friendly	✓
Disabled Facilities	-
Dog Friendly	-
Beer Garden	✓
Log Fire/Stove	✓
Storage Area	✓
Smoking in Bar	Separate smoking/non smoking areas
Food	Traditional and more adventurous dishes, all freshly prepared. Oriental Beef Salad £5.95, Cumberland Sausage £7.25
Beer (price per pint)	Pub has been given Cask Marque for Beer Quality. Timothy Taylors, Deuchars's, Boddingtons, as well as Beers from local breweries eg: Beckstones, Hawkshead, Hesket Newmarket, Jennings.
Guest Beers (price per pint)	-
Wine	-
Extras	Accommodation available

Blacksmith's Arms
Broughton Mills

Grid reference SD 222 905

Licensee	Michael and Sophie Lane
Brewery	Free House
Tel	01229 716824
Fax	✕
Email	blacksmithsarms@aol.com
Web	www.theblacksmithsarms.com
Description	Historic country pub set in the tranquil Lickle Valley. Open fires and small rooms offering cosy dining in a friendly atmosphere.
Summer Opening Hours	Mon 5pm – 11pm Tues – Sat 12am – 11pm (July to September) Sun 12am – 10.30pm
Winter Opening Hours	Mon 5pm –11pm Tues – Fri 12am – 2.30pm (October to June) 5pm – 11pm Sat 12am – 11pm Sun 12am – 10.30pm
Food Serving Times	Mon 6pm – 9pm Tues – Sun 12am – 2pm 6pm – 9pm
Child Friendly	Childrens' Menu
Disabled Facilities	✕
Dog Friendly	✓
Beer Garden	✓
Log Fire/Stove	✓
Storage Area	✓
Smoking in Bar	Separate smoking/non-smoking areas
Food	Award winning food using local ingredients, in particular Beef, Game, Fish and Herdwick Lamb. Guinea Fowl with a Smokey Bacon and Port Sauce £9.95, Beef Wellington with a Port and Shallot Sauce £9.95
Beer (price per pint)	Cumberland Ale, Hawkshead Bitter, Barngates Tag Lag, Dent Aviator, Slater's Original, Moorhouse's Pride of Pendle. All £1.95
Guest Beers (price per pint)	Ever changing
Wine	8 whites and 8 reds from £9.50

The Sun Hotel
Coniston

Grid reference SD 299 975

Licensee	Alan Piper
Brewery	Free House
Tel	015394 41248
Fax	015394 41219
Email	thesun@hotelconiston.com
Web	www.thesunconiston.com
Description	16th Century inn situated on the Walna Scar Road leading to Coniston Old Man. Exposed beams, flagstone floors and a welcoming old range in the fireplace.
Opening Hours	Mon – Sat 12pm –11pm Sun 12pm –10.30pm
Food Serving Times	12pm – 2.30pm 6pm –9pm
Child Friendly	Children's Menu
Disabled Facilities	✓
Dog Friendly	✓
Beer Garden	✓
Log Fire/Stove	✓
Storage Area	✓
Smoking in Bar	Separate smoking/non-smoking areas
Food	Homemade, fresh produce, locally sourced. Pink Roast Duck Breast £12.50, Loin of Venison £16
Beer (price per pint)	Coniston Bluebird £2.40, Hawkshead Bitter £2.30, Moorhouse's £2.20 - £2.40
Guest Beers (price per pint)	London Pride £2.40, Hawkshead Gold £2.40, Youngs Special £2.40, Adams Broadside £2.40, Black Sheep £2.40
Wine	30+ wine list from £11.50
Extras	10 traditionally furnished bedrooms £40 - £55/person/night. Dogs can stay for £4/night. Famous for its connections with Donald Cambell and his attempts at the Water Speed Record.

Black Bull Inn
Coniston

Grid reference SD 301 976

Licensee	Ronald E Bradley
Brewery	Coniston Brewing Co.
Tel	015394 41335
Fax	015394 41168
Email	✗
Web	www.conistonbrewery.com
Description	400 year old coaching inn situated in centre of the picturesque village of Coniston and in the shadow of The Old Man of Coniston.
Opening Hours	Mon – Sun 10am - 11pm
Food Serving Times	12pm – 9pm
Child Friendly	Children's Menu
Disabled Facilities	✓
Dog Friendly	✓
Beer Garden	✓
Log Fire/Stove	✓
Storage Area	✓
Smoking in Bar	Separate smoking/non-smoking areas
Food	Some local produce and homemade dishes. Daily specials, including vegetarian specials. Local Esthwaite Trout £8.95, Vegetable Moussaka £8.75
Beer (price per pint)	The pub has it's own micro brewery on-site. Coniston Bluebird Bitter £2.20, Coniston Bluebird XB £2.30, Coniston Old Man Ale £2.30, Coniston Blacksmith £2.60, Opium £2.25, Old Peculiar £2.60
Guest Beers (price per pint)	Timothy Taylors, Black Sheep, Thwaites
Wine	Wine list £13 - £19.25
Extras	The Coniston Brewing Company brew on site using natural ingredients and local mountain water. Bedrooms available

Sun Inn
Crook

Grid reference SD 464 951

Licensee	Mr Sykes
Brewery	Free House
Tel	01539 821351
Fax	X
Email	X
Web	X
Description	Traditional Inn with stone floors and open fires. Friendly Staff and welcoming atmosphere.
Opening Hours	Mon – Fri 12 – 2.30pm 6 –11pm Sat 12 – 11pm Sun 12 – 10.30pm
Food Serving Times	-
Child Friendly	-
Disabled Facilities	-
Dog Friendly	✓
Beer Garden	✓
Log Fire/Stove	✓
Storage Area	✓
Smoking in Bar	Smoking in Bar but not Restaurant
Food	Good mix of traditional and more exotic food. Cumbrian Fell Reared Ribeye Steak £11.95, Cumberland Sausage £8.95
Beer (price per pint)	Coniston Blue Bird, Theakstons Best Bitter, Speckled Hen, Old Peculiar, Courage Directors.
Guest Beers (price per pint)	-
Wine	Large Selection

The Punch Bowl Inn
Crosthwaite

Grid reference SD 446 912

Licensee	Stephen Carruthers
Brewery	Barngates
Tel	015395 68237
Fax	015395 68875
Email	info@the-punchbowl.co.uk
Web	www.the-punchbowl.co.uk
Description	Newly refurbished inn with restaurant style food. Cumbrian Dining Pub of the Year 2005.
Opening Hours	Mon – Sat 12am – 11pm Sun 12pm – 10.30pm
Food Serving Times	12pm – 3pm 6pm – 9pm
Child Friendly	Allowed in bar, but no children's menu
Disabled Facilities	✓
Dog Friendly	✓
Beer Garden	✓
Log Fire/Stove	✓
Storage Area	✓
Smoking in Bar	No smoking in Bar or Restaurant
Food	Locally sourced produce, organic where possible, not traditional pub fayre. Seared Calves Liver £12.75, Whole Roasted Pheasant £14.50
Beer (price per pint)	Beer from private brewery (Barngates) at sister pub The Drunken Duck, Ambleside. Tag Lag £2.25, Cat Nap £2.25, Lindeboom £2.60
Guest Beers (price per pint)	-
Wine	House wines £3.25 - £5.25 per glass
Extras	9 luxurious bedrooms available

Britannia Inn
Elterwater

Grid reference NY 327 048

Licensee	Clare Woodhead/Christopher Jones
Brewery	Free House
Tel	015394 37210
Fax	015394 37311
Email	info@britinn.co.uk
Web	www.britinn.co.uk
Description	This Inn is nearly 500 yrs old, with small, cosy, thick walled rooms, slate floors, oak beams and log fires. Large outdoor seating area in heart of the village.
Opening Hours	Mon – Sat 10am –11pm Sun 10am – 10.30 pm (All Year round)
Food Serving Times	12pm – 9.30pm (All year Round)
Child Friendly	Allowed in bar, but no children's menu
Disabled Facilities	X
Dog Friendly	✓
Beer Garden	✓
Log Fire/Stove	✓
Storage Area	✓
Smoking in Bar	Separate smoking/non-smoking areas
Food	Locally sourced, some organic produce. Local Lamb Shoulder £10.95, Homemade Pies £9.70
Beer (price per pint)	Coniston Bluebird £2.45, Jennings Bitter £2.30, Timothy Taylors Landlord £2.55
Guest Beers (price per pint)	2 guest beer pumps, changed every barrel Hawkshead Gold £2.40, Fraoch Britannia Inn Edition £2.50
Wine	Duc De Richelieu house wines £10.50, Yarra Valley Semillon Sauvignon £16.50, Merlot El Picador Chile £12
Extras	Annual Beer Festival

Wainwright's Inn
Chapel Stile

Grid reference NY 321 052

Licensee	Tina Darbyshire & Ben Clarke
Brewery	Free House
Tel	015394 38088
Fax	015394 38092
Email	wainwrightsinn@langdale.co.uk
Web	✗
Description	Created as an "authentic" Lakeland pub, has a welcoming atmosphere and friendly staff
Opening Hours	Mon – Fri 11.30am – 3pm 6pm 11pm Sat 11.30am – 11pm Sun 12pm – 10.30pm
Food Serving Times	Mon – Sat 12 – 2pm 6pm –9pm Sun 12 - 2.30pm 6 – 9pm
Child Friendly	Children's menu
Disabled Facilities	✗
Dog Friendly	✓
Beer Garden	✓
Log Fire/Stove	✓
Storage Area	✓
Smoking in Bar	Separate smoking/non-smoking areas
Food	Large portions of traditional pub food. Wainwright's Lamb £9.25, Mushroom & Spinach Lasagne £7.95
Beer (price per pint)	Jennings Bitter £2.20, Jennings Cumberland £2.40, Jennings Snecklifter £2.65, Boddingtons £2.65
Guest Beers (price per pint)	Guest beers from local breweries (Barngates, Blacksheep, Hesket Newmarket) all £2.45
Wine	12 wines from £11.50
Extras	Quiz nite every Tuesday

Tweedies Bar
Grasmere

Grid reference NY 336 074

Licensee	Mr Brian Roberts
Brewery	Free House
Tel	015394 35300
Fax	015394 35570
Email	enquiries@dalelodgehotel.co.uk
Web	www.dalelodgehotel.co.uk
Description	A more modern style bar, with a welcoming atmosphere and a large beer garden.
Opening Hours	Mon – Sat 11am – 1am Sun 12am -1am
Food Serving Times	Mon – Sat 12am – 3pm 6pm – 9pm Sun 12am – 4pm 6.30pm – 9pm
Child Friendly	Children's menu
Disabled Facilities	✗
Dog Friendly	✓
Beer Garden	✓
Log Fire/Stove	✓
Storage Area	✓
Smoking in Bar	Separate smoking/non-smoking areas
Food	Local fresh produce. Homemade Steak & Ale Pie £10.95, Whole Roast Seabass £13.95, Pizzas served (takeaway available) 8.30pm – 10pm
Beer (price per pint)	Jennings Bitter £2.20, Jennings Cumberland £2.40, Jennings Snecklifter £2.65, Boddingtons £2.65
Guest Beers (price per pint)	Extensive range of guest ales, changing weekly. £2.60/pint Timothy Taylors Landlord, Coniston Bluebird, Bitter & Twisted, Skull Splitter, Deuchars IPA
Wine	Varied wine selection from £11.95 - £145
Extras	Sunday Lunches 12 – 4pm, 2 courses £10.95, 3 courses £13.95, children under 8 eat free. Restaurant open to residents and non-residents for dinner 7 days a week

King's Arms Hotel
Hawkshead

Grid reference SD 352 982

Licensee	Ed & Lee Johnson
Brewery	Free House
Tel	015394 36372
Fax	015394 36006
Email	info@kingsarmshawkshead.co.uk
Web	www.kingsarmshawkshead.co.uk
Description	Small, friendly pub in The Square in Hawkshead village.
Opening Hours	Mon – Sun 11am – 11pm
Food Serving Times	12pm – 2.30pm 6pm – 9.30pm
Child Friendly	Children's menu
Disabled Facilities	✓
Dog Friendly	✓ (dogs allowed in bedrooms too!)
Beer Garden	✓
Log Fire/Stove	✓
Storage Area	✓
Smoking in Bar	Separate smoking/non-smoking areas
Food	Ingredients sourced locally, some organic produce used, free from GM. Vegetarian Quiche of the Day £6.95, Cumberland Sausage £7.25
Beer (price per pint)	Hawkshead Bitter £1.90, Hawkshead Gold £2.05, Coniston Bluebird £2.20, Black Sheep £2.15
Guest Beers (price per pint)	Moorhouse's, Copper Dragon, Hesket Newmarket, York.
Wine	Wine list from £9.50 – £28.95
Extras	Annual Trail Running events, new to Hawkshead in 2006 Bedrooms £38, self catering cottages available too.

The Watermill Inn
Ings

Grid reference SD 445 986

Licensee	Brian Coulthwaite
Brewery	Free House
Tel	01539 821309
Fax	01539 822309
Email	all@watermillinn.co.uk
Web	www.watermillinn.co.uk
Description	A former wood mill converted to a traditional inn situated in the quiet backwater of Ings. Still retains some original features and is full of character.
Opening Hours	Mon – Sat 12pm - 11pm Sun 12pm - 10.30pm
Food Serving Times	12pm – 4.30pm 5pm – 9pm
Child Friendly	Children's menu
Disabled Facilities	✓
Dog Friendly	allowed in one bar only
Beer Garden	✓
Log Fire/Stove	✓
Storage Area	✗
Smoking in Bar	Separate smoking/non-smoking areas
Food	Local ingredients providing a broad range of local dishes and continental cuisine. Beef & Bluebrid Ale Pie £8.25, Local 10oz Rump Steak £12.75
Beer (price per pint)	Coniston Blue Bird, Theakstons Best, Blacksheep Best Bitter, Black Sheep Special, Hawkshead Bitter, Theakstons Old Peculiar, JW Lees Moonraker, Moorhouse's Black Cat (£2.10 - £2.90)
Guest Beers (price per pint)	Duechars IPA £2.10, Orkney Park Island £2.30, Yates Fever Pitch £2.20, Smiles Blond £2.10, Hesket Newmarket Special £2.30, Jennings Cumberland Ale £2.10
Wine	Mills Reef Sauv Blanc £12.50, Caliterra Merlot £11.95
Extras	In Early 2006, The Watermill Inn will be hosting their own beer, brewed on site, all named with a dog theme! Story Telling Club meets once a month.

Three Shires Inn
Little Langdale

Grid reference NY 316 034

Licensee	Ian Stephenson
Brewery	Free House
Tel	015394 37215
Fax	015394 37127
Email	enquiry@threeshiresinn.co.uk
Web	www.threeshiresinn.co.uk
Description	Family run inn set in picturesque surroundings.
Opening Hours – Summer	Mon – Sat 11am-10.30pm (11pm Sat) Sun 12pm – 10.30pm
Opening Hours – Winter	Mon-Sun 11am – 3pm 8pm – 10.30pm
Food Serving Times	12pm –6.45pm (Limited evening meals in Dec and Jan. Please telephone to check)
Child Friendly	Children's menu
Disabled Facilities	✗
Dog Friendly	✓
Beer Garden	✓
Log Fire/Stove	✓
Storage Area	✓
Smoking in Bar	Currently in one bar only, after 9.30pm (may change to non smoking in 2007)
Food	Locally sourced fresh produce, all freshly prepared meals. Cumberland Sausage £7.95, Beef & Ale Pie £7.95
Beer (price per pint)	Jennings Best £2.30, Hawkshead Best £2.50, Cumberland Ale £2.40
Guest Beers (price per pint)	Coniston Old Man £2.60
Wine	4 House Wines £11.50 Plus 30+ wine list
Extras	Bedrooms £72

Outgate Inn
Outgate

Grid reference SD 354 998

Licensee	Tony Gray
Brewery	F. Robinson Ltd
Tel	015394 36413
Fax	✗
Email	outgate@outgate.wanadoo.co.uk
Web	✗
Description	Traditional, friendly village pub.
Opening Hours – Feb to Oct	Mon – Fri 11am – 3pm 6pm – 11pm
	Sat 11am – 11pm Sun 12pm – 10.30pm
Opening Hours – Nov to Feb	Mon – Sat 12 –2.30pm 6-11pm Sun 12 – 2.30pm 7 – 10.30pm
	(Opening times over the Christmas period may vary,
	please telephone to check)
Food Serving Times	12 – 2pm 6pm – 9pm (7pm - 9pm Sundays in Winter)
Child Friendly	Children's menu
Disabled Facilities	✗
Dog Friendly	✓
Beer Garden	✓
Log Fire/Stove	✓
Storage Area	✗
Smoking in Bar	Separate smoking/non-smoking areas
Food	A mix of traditional and non-traditional pub food.
	Tempura Vegetables £7.95, Grilled Scottish Salmon £9.95
Beer (price per pint)	Hartley's XB £2.20, Robinson's Smooth £2.30, Old Stockport £2.10
Guest Beers (price per pint)	Double Hop £2.30
Wine	Up a Gum Tree Shiraz £11.95, Jean Paul Rouge £12.95
Extras	Live Jazz every Friday from Feb to Nov

Newfield Inn
Seathwaite

Grid reference SD 227 960

Licensee	Paul Batten
Brewery	Free House
Tel	01229 716208
Fax	✗
Email	✗
Web	www.newfieldinn.co.uk
Description	Wonderfully remote but bustling inn in Wordsworth's favourite valley. Warm, friendly atmosphere and a unique slate floor.
Opening Hours	Mon – Sun 11am – 11pm (10.30pm on Sundays)
Food Serving Times	12pm – 9pm
Child Friendly	Children's menu and play area
Disabled Facilities	✗
Dog Friendly	✓
Beer Garden	✓
Log Fire/Stove	✓
Storage Area	✓
Smoking in Bar	Separate smoking/non-smoking areas
Food	Fresh meat locally sourced from Irvings of Ulverston or Meville Tyson of Broughton. Herdwick Lamb from Langdale. Homemade Steak Pie £7.95, Homemade Spicy Bean Casserole (V) £5.95
Beer (price per pint)	Theakstons Old Peculiar £2.50, Jennings Cumberland Ale £2.00, Caledonian Deuchars IPA £2.00
Guest Beers (price per pint)	Ever changing guest beers
Wine	Several wines for £9.95
Extras	Annual Fell race in June, Broughton Beer Festival in October

Eagle & Child Inn
Staveley

Grid reference SD 471 981

Licensee	Richard & Denise Coleman
Brewery	Free House
Tel	01539 821320
Fax	X
Email	info@eaglechildinn.co.uk
Web	www.eaglechildinn.co.uk
Description	Riverside beer garden. Warm, welcoming bar with large rustic wooden tables.
Opening Hours	11am – 11pm
Food Serving Times	Mon – Fri 12pm – 2.30pm 6pm –9pm
	Sat – Sun 12pm – 3pm 6pm – 9pm
Child Friendly	Children's Menu
Disabled Facilities	X
Dog Friendly	✓
Beer Garden	✓
Log Fire/Stove	✓
Storage Area	✓
Smoking in Bar	Separate smoking/non-smoking areas
Food	All local produce. Staveley Sausages £8.25, Kentmere Lamb Hotpot £8.50
Beer (price per pint)	Barngates £2.20, Tirril £2.20, Yates £2.20, Black Sheep £2.20, Hawkshead £2.30, Tetley £2
Guest Beers (price per pint)	Many varying guest ales/lagers/ciders
Wine	-
Extras	Beer festival every quarter. Beamed function room, en-suite bedrooms.

The Mason's Arms
Strawberry Bank

Grid reference SD 413 894

Licensee	John Taylor
Brewery	Free House
Tel	015395 68486
Fax	015395 68780
Email	info@masonsarms.info
Web	www.strawberrybank.com
Description	A traditional 16th century fellside pub with outstanding views over the Winster valley. Attractive outdoor seating in front and a warm, friendly interior.
Opening Hours – April to Oct	Mon – Sat 11.30am – 11pm Sun 12pm – 10.30pm
Opening Hours – Nov to Mar	Mon – Fri 11.30am – 3pm 6pm – 11pm Sat 11.30am – 11pm Sun 12pm – 10.30pm
Food Serving Times	Mon – Sat 12pm – 2pm 6pm - 9pm Sun 12pm – 3pm 6pm – 8pm
Child Friendly	Children's Menu
Disabled Facilities	✗
Dog Friendly	✗
Beer Garden	✓
Log Fire/Stove	✓
Storage Area	✗
Smoking in Bar	Separate smoking/non-smoking areas
Food	Wide range of local produce including ales, meats and cheeses. Seasonally changing menu. Cullen Skink £6.25, Cumbrian Duck Sausage Salad £6.25
Beer (price per pint)	Black Sheep £2.30, Hawkshead £2.30, Timothy Taylor Landlord £2.50, Leffe £3.60. Over 50 imported bottled beers Locally brewed. Damson Beer £3.25/btl
Guest Beers (price per pint)	Hawkshead Red £2.50, Timothy Taylor Golden Best £2.50
Wine	Wide range of wines by bottle or glass. Marques De Riscal Sauv Blanc £12.50

Mortal Man
Troutbeck

Grid reference NY 410 034

Licensee	Nick Drew & Paul Riley
Brewery	Enterprise Inns
Tel	015394 33193
Fax	01539431261
Email	themortalman@msn.com
Web	www.themortalman.co.uk
Description	Wonderfully positioned 16th Century building. Beer garden has fantastic views along the tranquil Troutbeck Valley.
Opening Hours	11am – 11pm
Food Serving Times	12pm – 3pm 6pm – 9pm
Child Friendly	Children's Menu
Disabled Facilities	✗
Dog Friendly	✓
Beer Garden	✓
Log Fire/Stove	✓
Storage Area	✓
Smoking in Bar	Separate smoking/non-smoking areas
Food	Locally sourced produce. Homemade Soup £2.75, Venison Sausages £8
Beer (price per pint)	Theakstons Best £2.20, Jennings Cumberland £2.45
Guest Beers (price per pint)	Green King IPA, Black Sheep, Lancaster Blonde, all £2.80
Wine	Bottles from £12.75
Extras	12 bedrooms available

Queen's Head Hotel
Troutbeck

Grid reference NY 414 038

Licensee	Mark Stewardson
Brewery	Free House
Tel	015394 32174
Fax	015394 31938
Email	enquiries@queensheadhotel.com
Web	www.queensheadhotel.com
Description	17th Century Coaching Inn with bar made from a four poster bed from Appleby Castle, solid oak beams, flagstone floors and log fires.
Opening Hours	Mon – Sat 11am – 11pm　　Sun 12pm – 10.30pm
Food Serving Times	12pm – 2pm 6.30pm – 8.45pm
Child Friendly	Children's Menu
Disabled Facilities	✓
Dog Friendly	✓
Beer Garden	✓
Log Fire/Stove	✓
Storage Area	✓
Smoking in Bar	Separate smoking/non-smoking areas
Food	Locally sourced produce, homemade dishes. Homemade Pork & Stilton Sausages £7.50, Fillet of Smoked Haddock £7.95
Beer (price per pint)	Jennings Best, Coniston Bluebird, Tirril, Blacksheep, Hawkshead £2 - £2.50
Guest Beers (price per pint)	Barngates £2.50
Wine	Wine List from £12.50 - £21.95
Extras	Accommodation available

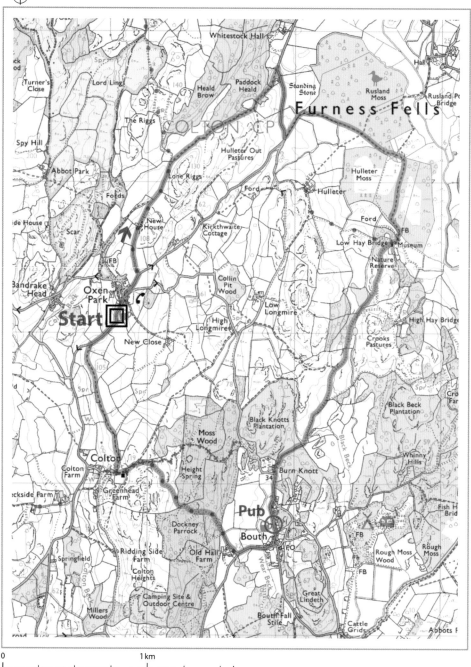

walk 1 Bouth

distance: 5.5 miles | time: 2½ hours | Start Grid Ref: SD 317 871

level: easy | terrain: pasture, moss and woodland

START

1. Park in lay-by just outside Oxen Park on the road to Colton (or in village). From Oxen Park village, walk up the road in the direction of *Rusland, Grizedale and Hawkshead*. A short distance along the road, turn left on to a narrow lane, marked *"unsuitable for motor vehicles"*. Continue past the white cottage and the tarmac lane becomes a stony track.

2. Before reaching the gate, take the footpath off to the right, through a kissing gate, into a field. Follow the track as it runs parallel to the wall on your right. Enter the woods through a kissing gate and follow the short path to a wooden gate leading into an open field. Walk down the hill and continue along the track, bearing left towards the next wooded copse.

3. Go through the gate and follow the track through the woods. Leave the woods by a kissing gate and walk through the shady paddock at the back of a house. Take the gate on the right, then turn right on to the tarmac lane (in the field to the left of you is a large Standing Stone on the crest of a small hill).

4. Just before the lane takes a sharp turn to the right (signposted *Colton, Ulverston*), cross the stream by a small wooden bridge on your left and take the public footpath through the gate into the field. Follow the path along the right hand side of the stream (sometimes boggy) to a stile in the bottom right hand corner. Cross the stile into Rusland Moss, taking care to keep to the path as there are deep boggy areas to both sides.

5. You soon come to a bridge on the right over a waterway (signposted left to *Rusland Pool*, right to *Hulleter Farm*). Do not cross the bridge but carry straight on, following the path alongside the waterway. Keep to the yellow arrows through the moss, then, at the wooden walkway crossing your path, turn right.

6. The next area of the moss is slightly firmer under foot. Keep to the path and eventually you cross a wooden bridge. Go through a gate and out onto a track. Turn left and follow the footpath signs through a kissing gate and across the yard in front of a white cottage (Low Hay Barn). Follow the drive up the hill, and continue along the tarmac lane for about 1 mile, leaving the nature reserve.

7. At the end of the lane turn left and into the village of Bouth. As you reach the road junction, the White Hart is on your right.

PUB - White Hart see full pub details on page 14

8. From the White Hart turn right up the lane towards *Greenodd, Ulverston* and *Coniston*, past the phone box and over the bridge. Just out of the village, turn right up the drive to Old Hall Farm (no sign outside the farm). Keep to the right hand track past the farm and continue up into Dockney Parrock Woods. Follow the main track up the hill, then through a wooden gate out of the woodland.

9. Carry on over the hill (with views of the Lakeland fells ahead) and drop down to the church at Colton, through a gate out of the field. Take the footpath on your right, opposite the churchyard. A few yards on, as the wire fence meets the wall, go through a kissing gate (1) on the left. Follow the wall on your right, then through another kissing gate (2). Turn left now, following the wall on your left. At the wire fence, go

Rusland Moss

Rusland Moss Nature Reserve covers 58 acres and is managed by the Lake District National Park Authority. It is the northern part of one of the last remaining raised mires (peat bogs) in the country.

through yet another kissing gate (3) and continue to follow the wall on your left. Go through kissing gate number 4 and follow the path round the hill, parallel with the road below.

10. As you round the hill, Oxen Park village is straight ahead of you. Drop down the hill slightly and leave the field via the wooden gate. Turn right on to the lane and continue up to the village.

FINISH

The Black Beck Gunpowder Works

On the 25th July 1868 nine men were killed and many others injured at Black Beck in what turned out to be the worst accident in the history of local gunpowder manufacture. It was a dangerous business and gunpowder works were deliberately located in remote and undulating areas like this, often with access to water power, though in this case steam engines were used from the very beginning.

Black Beck was one of several sites in South Lakeland where gunpowder was produced in large quantities in the 18th and 19th centuries. Between them, seven works supplied the bulk of the country's need for the 'black powder'. It was used by the military, the navy and for blasting in mines and quarries. The works was eventually taken over by Nobel Explosives, later part of ICI. The works closed in 1928. It is now a caravan park.

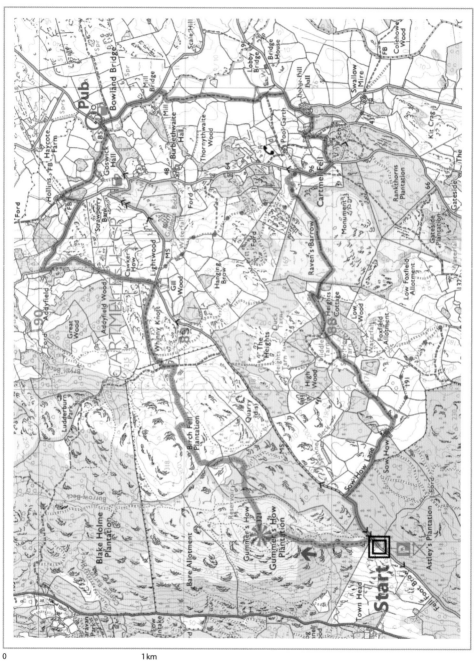

0   1km

0   1 mile   Scale 1:25000

walk 2 Bowland Bridge

distance: **7 miles** | time: **4 hours** | Start Grid Ref: **SD 389 876**

level: **moderate** | terrain: **pasture and forest**

START

1. Park in Forestry Commission (FC) car park at Gummer's Howe picnic site. Turn right up the road from the car park and in a few yards take the footpath on the left signposted to *Gummer's Howe Summit*. Climb the hill following the rocky path, taking in views of Lake Windermere and the hills beyond.

2. From the cairn on the summit of Gummer's Howe, take the broad green path going north-east, which bends round to the right, towards the nearest clump of trees and swings down the hillside. After 50 yards or so (as you turn to face south), turn left down a narrow grassy path towards the forest. At a wire fence, cross over the stile and into a coniferous wood.

3. The path descends through tall conifers to a reservoir, and then bends round the right. At a concrete dam, continue round the edge of the reservoir, through the woods, negotiating a stream and boggy area of ground. Cross another small stream to join a broader path.

4. Turn left after the green man marker (Forestry Commission marker posts) to join a path that gently ascends through mature conifers. Pass the northern end of the reservoir and an area of open reedy ground to your left. The path rises into more woodland, with the remnants of a drystone wall on your right.

5. At a Forestry Commission (FC) marker post, the path curves to the right along the course of a small stream. Where the stream forks to the left, continue up through the trees, then climb the steep bank, which brings you to a clearing on top of the hill. Here, another FC post shows the route into a dark forest.

6. After several twists and turns you join a broad path with a stream running alongside, as it descends through the woods. The broad track continues through a more recent plantation of conifers, and you cross the stream as it curves away to the left. Where the track broadens again, you join another wide track coming up from the right. Turn left here onto the broad track, following the yellow arrows.

7. A few yards after crossing a stream, three yellow arrows indicate the footpaths. Turn right and walk past the tumbled-down stone building. Climb the stile over the wall into open pasture (you may have to negotiate the boggy area immediately in front of you). The path heads to the left, between the wall and the rocky hill. Descend the hill towards the road and a sign for *Lightwood Country Guesthouse*.

Cartmel Fell Church

The church was built as a "Chapel of Ease" in about 1505, literally to make life easier for the local inhabitants and save them the long journey to the mother church at Cartmel. It is the only church in the north of England dedicated to St Anthony whose patron saint portfolio included swineherds, lost things and charcoal burners – perhaps this last is the local connection as charcoal burning was once extensive and is still carried out in the area.

Inside the church at the end of the nave are two elaborate enclosed pews. On the north side is the Cowmire Hall pew, thought to have been made out of the Rood Screen after the Reformation. This probably served as an early 'schoolroom' for local children. On the other side, and from about the same period, is the Burblethwaite Hall pew. The rare 3-decker pulpit was made in 1698 – the lower deck for the clerk, the middle deck for the reader and the top deck was where the sermon was preached (and still is).

8. Go through the gate and turn left up the tarmac lane. At a white cottage, turn right towards *Bowland Bridge*. Follow the lane down the hill for around $1/2$ mile, and then turn left down the first driveway, onto a public bridleway to *Hollins Farm*.

9. Go through the gate and follow the drive down towards the white cottage. Just before the cottage, follow a white marker through a small wooden gate to your right. After a few yards pass through another small gate into open pasture. Turn right, and keeping the woodland on your right, go straight ahead to a stile. Cross the field to a stile with a yellow arrow, set between two trees. Goswick Hall is on your right.

10. Follow the yellow markers through the field and into a copse of trees on the right. Go through the kissing gate and follow the path winding through the trees. Leave the woods at the far side and then cross the field towards a drystone wall. Go through the kissing gate by the stream and then turn left on to road, over Bowland Bridge. The Hare & Hounds is ahead of you.

PUB - Hare & Hounds
see full pub details on page 15

11. From the pub, turn left, retracing your steps a short way, then turn left between the white cottages, signposted to *Witherslack*. A few yards after the entrance to Burblethwaite Mill, take a footpath on the right. Cross over the stile, through the small field and then over a small wooden bridge. Turn left after the bridge, towards a gate in the far left hand corner of the field.

12. Cross over the stile in the wall next to the gate, then bear left across the field to a stile in a wire fence. Turn right after the stile, along the field boundary to a small wooden gate, just before a hawthorne hedge on the right (easily missed). Turn left and follow the hedge along to a gated stile, then continue with the hedge now to your right.

13. Through another stile, across the stream, bear left for a few yards, then follow the wall to your right. Go through the next wooden gate and follow the path along the hedge on your left. Go through the gate and turn right onto a tarmac road.

14. As you reach the buildings of Hodge Hall (the first on the left), continue up the hill towards *High Newton* and *Cartmel*. At the end of the buildings of Hodge Hall, turn right onto a footpath into mixed woodland. At the top of the wood, cross over the stile onto a small grassy track leading into the churchyard to the left. Go through the iron gate to the left of the church then turn right in front of the church and take the footpath up the hill towards the woods. Go into the wood following the path to the road.

15. Turn right onto the road and as it descends, turn left into a gateway, opposite two gates on the other side of the road. Follow the broad bridle-path up the hill, then take the left hand track on to the bridleway to *Sow How*. Keep to the track, bearing right as it crosses the fell. Where the path reaches a wider grassy track, bear right and follow the bridle-path to a wooden gate next to woodland. Go through the gate and continue up towards the stone barn. Follow the track to the right of the barn and round the sharp left hand corner into the next field. Continue through the gateway and into the woods. At the end of the woods pass through another gate and descend the hill with Sow How tarn on the right hand side. Walk past the foot of the tarn to a gate in a wire fence. Follow the bridleway to the farm, go through the yard and up the track to the road. Turn left on to the road and follow it as it drops down the hill. The car park is on your left.

FINISH

N

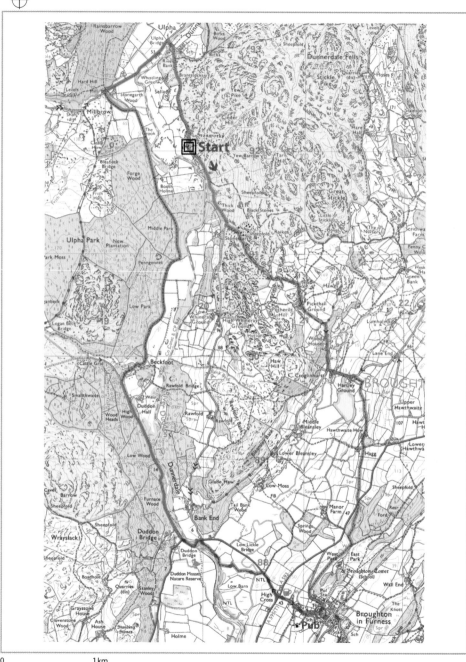

walk 3 Broughton-in-Furness

distance: 9 miles | time: 4$\frac{1}{2}$ hours | Start Grid Ref: SD 198 919

level: strenuous | terrain: pasture, rough fell and woodland

START

1. Park in the old quarry on the right hand side of the road between Duddon Bridge and Ulpha (roughly 3 miles from Duddon Bridge). From the car park, walk south down the road for $\frac{1}{4}$ mile (river to your right) then take the bridleway on the left, opposite Stone Star turning place. The track winds steeply up the craggy hill.

2. At the top, follow the path to the left of the stream. Where the stream dries up and the ground levels out, two tracks come in from the left. Take the second of the two tracks and then the right fork off this track, towards a gate in a drystone wall. There is a large boggy area of ground to your right.

3. Go through the gate and turn left between the wall and the crag. Bear right to round the crag, and join a track heading down the hill along the wall. At the gate, turn right following the track parallel with the wall on the right down to the farm. Go through the gate, then turn left in front of the white and yellow house and through a second gate on to a broad track heading down the hill.

4. At the end of the track turn right down the shady lane. At the bottom of the hill turn left and follow the road between the farm buildings. Cross over High Lickle Bridge and walk up the lane past the next house. Just after the house take the footpath on your right, through the stile into the field, then over a second stile onto a narrow path to the side of an orchard.

5. Climb the next stile into the field, and head towards the gap in the wall next to a large tree. Follow the wall on your right to the top right corner and pass over a stile. Follow the row of trees in the same direction towards the house, then along a wider track through a wooded area to the rear of the house and out into a field. Follow the fence on your left to a wooden gate and across a stream onto a tarmac lane.

6. Cross straight over the lane and climb the stile into the field in front of you. Head across the field to a stile in the wall. Follow the hedge along, over another stile, continuing through this next field in the same direction. Continue through the next field and round the hill slightly, towards a stile onto the road.

7. Turn right down the road, then immediately left over a stile. Bear right through the field, over the stream and follow the faint path parallel to the road until you come to a track leading from a substantial gateway to your right. Follow the track to the left, then as the track reaches the private land of Broughton Tower, go over the distinctive iron ladder stile into the field on the right.

8. Keeping the fenced off pond to the right, walk through the field and follow the path round the hill to a small gate in the fence leading onto the road. Turn left down the road into Broughton. Just before the Obelisk in the market square, turn right and walk straight on to the Old Kings Head.

PUB - Old King's Head see full pub details on page 16

9. From the pub, head out of the town towards *Ulpha* and *Millom*. At the High Cross junction, turn right, crossing the road carefully, and walk down the grass verge. 200 yards down the road, take the footpath to the left (signposted *Duddon Bridge $1/2$ mile*), along a track and across the small bridge, going through the gate into the field. Follow the wall straight ahead through the field. At the far side of the field, go through the metal gate on to a broader path that follows the River Duddon round to the right. Go through the next gate up to the main road.

Sir Thomas Broughton & Lambert Simnel

In the late 1400's, Sir Thomas Broughton, who lived at Broughton Tower, was closely involved in an ill-fated attempt to seize the crown from Henry VII and as a result lost his lands and (probably) his life.

The Wars of the Roses ended with the defeat of Richard III at the Battle of Bosworth in 1485 and success for the House of Lancaster and Henry Tudor. The years immediately following the crowning of Henry VII saw a continuing struggle between York and Lancaster and in 1487 Margaret, Duchess of Burgundy, sister to the late Richard III, inaugurated a false claim to the throne involving a boy little more than 10 or 12 years old, called Lambert Simnel.

The boy was coached in this enterprise to impersonate the Earl of Warwick (a son of Edward IV), whom Henry had locked in the Tower. Margaret supplied an army of 2000 German mercenaries and together they landed in Ireland. There he was hailed as the rightful King of England and was crowned in Dublin in May 1487.

Under the command of an experienced soldier, Martin Swart, the army, now swollen by several thousand Irishmen, crossed the Irish Sea and landed at Piel Island, close to Barrow in Furness. They proceeded to Swarthmoor, near Ulverston, where they were joined by Sir Thomas Broughton and several other disaffected English nobles and their retinues. The plan was to cross the Pennines to York and, gathering support on the way, to march on London.

The people of York were unconvinced, however, and the march south failed to swell the army much at all. They met the forces of Henry near Newark, at the village of Stoke, where they were slaughtered in their thousands. It is uncertain as to whether Sir Thomas met his end on the battlefield or, as one account puts it, "he survived the battle and found asylum among his tenants at Witherslack, where, dying in seclusion in 1495, the family became extinct." Henry gave his lands to the Stanley family.

The young Lambert was taken prisoner at the battle but, being still a child, was spared execution. Instead, he was taken into the service of the royal kitchen and put to work as a menial. There is no evidence to suggest that he eventually found his true vocation in the making of cakes.

10. Turn left along the road, over the bridge, being careful with the traffic as there is no pavement. Shortly after the bridge turn right up the road to Corney Fell. Walk along this road through the woods for about a mile (there is no pavement here either, although the traffic is minimal), past two private driveways for Duddon Hall on the right hand side.

11. ¹/₂ mile after the second driveway to Duddon Hall is a footpath down a driveway on the right, signposted to *Broughton Mills and Ulpha*. Follow the drive down between the cottages and over the stone bridge. At the outbuildings close to the river, follow the main track bearing left slightly into the woodland. This track follows the course of the River Duddon for almost 2 miles through woodland.

12. Continue along the track out into pasture until it reaches the road. Turn right down the road towards Ulpha. Take the first road on the right, over the bridge and follow it for ¹/₂ mile back to the quarry car park.

FINISH

N

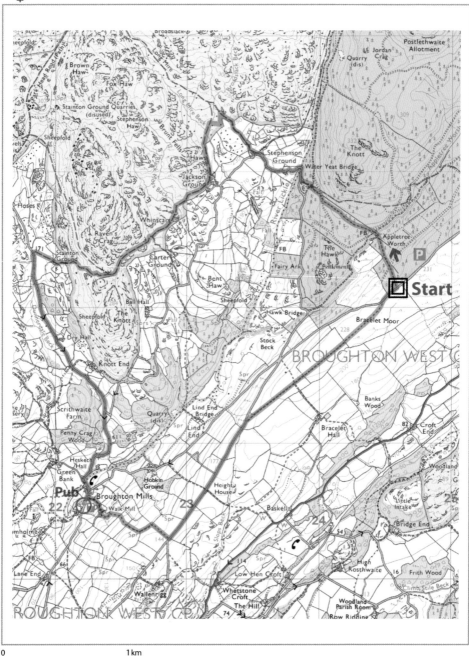

walk 4 Broughton Mills

distance: 6.6 miles | time: 3½ hours | Start Grid Ref: SD 245 921

level: moderate | terrain: pasture, fell and woodland

START

1. Park on Broughton Moor near the Forestry Commission sign. Take the footpath on the same side heading into the woods, signposted *Appletree Worth ¼ mile*. Follow the narrow path through the trees and down the slope to an area of open ground. Walk straight ahead down the hill, following the faint path towards the stone wall, ignoring the wide track to the right. Cross the marshy area towards the tumbled stone buildings of Appletree Worth settlement via the log path (may be slippy, some logs submerged and unstable!).

2. Cross the stream behind the stone buildings via the stepping-stones, then head up the bank into the trees. At the wide vehicle track go straight on, following the yellow arrows along a path through the woods.

3. At the far side of the woodland turn right on to a wide logging track. After 100

yards, turn left on to a footpath running between a larch plantation and a stone wall. At the yellow markers (pointing right and left), cross the track and join the bridle-path ahead of you into the woods. Go through the gate, then, after 50 yards or so, turn right onto a narrow tarmac lane.

4. Cross over the bridge (River Lickle) and follow the lane up the hill. At Stephenson's Ground, shortly after the first stone barn on the right, go through a wooden gate onto a bridle-path. Take the left hand track, signposted *Seathwaite*. The track soon becomes a walled green lane. Continue along the lane through two gates. At the second gate turn left and follow the wall through more open fell. As the wall turns sharply to the left, follow the narrow path to cut the corner and rejoin the wall further on, in front of the hill.

5. Bear left towards the farm, following the path along the wall behind the farm buildings. The path continues for around two miles, with fantastic views across to the Duddon Estuary straight ahead, and a steady climb up Raven's Crag to your right.

6. At the top of the hill as the track levels out, take the left-hand fork heading down a steep and winding gully to a wooden gate. Go through the gate and down the grassy lane, passing the derelict barns, through the field and out through a metal gate onto a tarmac lane. Turn left and follow the lane for around 1 mile down the valley to Broughton Mills. In the Village, cross over the bridge and continue round the corner, past the red phone box. The Blacksmith's Arms is a few yards up the lane, on the right hand side.

PUB - Blacksmith's Arms

see full pub details on page 17

7. From the pub walk back down the road and take the footpath to *Baskell, 3/4 mile,* on the right just before the first house. Follow the broad lane up the hill, then turn right onto a grassy path running directly behind the house. A few yards on, take a sharp left up a grassy bank following the yellow markers. Climb the stile and go through the trees out into a field.

Charles Kempe

Holy Innocents church at Broughton Mills contains a stained glass window (Christ on the Cross) by Charles Kempe, a renowned artist in glass whose speciality was the use of silver stain. Born near Brighton in 1837, most of his stained glass church work was carried out in the 1860's, produced in his London workshops. There are a dozen or so churches in Cumbria with a Kempe window, but his work can be seen in many parts of the country.

He is credited with perfecting the use of silver stain on clear glass – a yellow tint develops ranging from delicate to deep, depending on the amount of stain used. He was greatly influenced by the stained glass of Northern Germany and the Low Countries, produced in the 16th century.

The window is behind the altar and is a memorial to Frederic Amadeus Malleson, vicar of Holy Innocents from 1870 to 1897. The small wheatsheaf symbol, characteristic of the Kempe studio, appears in the bottom left hand corner.

8. Head up the field, bearing left slightly, and go through a metal gate in the hedge. Go straight up the next field and through a small kissing gate next to a larger gate. Follow the line of trees up the field, then go through a wooden gate and out into another field. Turn left and follow the wall along to the wooden fence. Cross over the stile, then follow the hedge up the hill to a metal gate. Turn left on the tarmac lane and continue along it for around 3/4 of a mile.

9. As the lane begins to gently drop down the hill and bend to the left slightly, bear right onto a footpath, over the stile in the wall to the right of a metal gate, signposted *Bracelet Moor*. Follow this broad track along the top of Bracelet Moor for about 1 mile, heading in the same direction all the time. Pass through a gateway and continue along the track towards a ladder stile and the lane running alongside the forest of Broughton Moor. Climb the ladder stile and turn right onto the lane to find yourself back at the car park.

FINISH

N

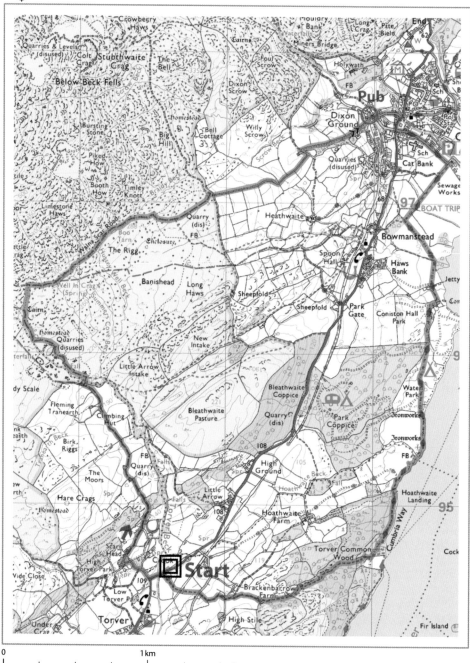

0		1km
0		1 mile

Scale 1:25000

walk 5 Coniston

distance: 7 miles | time: 3$\frac{1}{2}$ hours | Start Grid Ref: SD 285 945

level: moderate | terrain: rocky tracks, lakeside paths

START

1. Park on the Coniston side of Torver on the A593 in one of two lay-bys. Walk along the road towards Torver, cross over the bridge and then turn right up the lane following the sign to Crook Barn Stables and the footpath sign *Walna Scar/Coniston Old Man.*

2. Bearing left as you walk up the hill, follow the tarmac road past Crook Barn and Scar Head Cottage; the lane then bends to the right and joins the bridleway to Walna Scar. After the last house on the left, the lane turns into a walled rocky track. After a short distance, the track passes through a wooden gate and begins a gentle ascent.

3. Go through a second gate with a stone barn to the left. Shortly after the barn, turn right, following the bridleway through more open country. At the climbing hut/cottage pass through the gate and bear right over the concrete bridge (Tranearth Beck) towards the slate/slag heaps. Follow the blue arrows through more gates then cross over Torver Beck by a wooden bridge. Turn left in front of the slate heaps along the side of the beck.

4. The path ascends onto open fell with Torver Beck on your left. At the waterfall into a disused quarry, continue straight on towards Coniston Old Man. The faint remnants of a homestead are situated to the right of the path. Take the right hand fork before the path begins a steeper climb. Cross over the stream and continue past an old kiln on the right. Where the path forks again, bear right. A few yards ahead, turn right on to the wide rocky track of the Walna Scar Road.

5. Follow the track for $1/2$ mile, past the car park and through a metal gate onto a tarmac lane. The lane descends steeply for about $1/2$ mile down into the village of Coniston. As the road enters the village turn left and the Sun Hotel is a few yards down on the left hand side.

PUB - Sun Hotel see full pub details on page 18

6. From the pub walk down the hill towards the village. At the junction turn right and cross the road. Shortly after the BP Garage turn left on to Lake Road. Walk down towards the lake past the John Ruskin School on your right. At the sharp left hand bend in the road, take the footpath on your right over a stile, or through the gates, into the field. This is signposted to *Torver and the Lake Side Path*. Follow the well-defined path through the fields and towards Coniston Hall at the edge of the lake.

7. At Coniston Hall the path joins a tarmac drive. Continue in front of the hall and on through the campsite. Keep to the main drive, then as the road forks, bear left and follow the yellow footpath arrow off the tarmac drive down to the lake. Go through the gate and continue along the lakeside path, with exceptional views across Coniston Water. The site of an old ironworks/bloomery can be seen in this field, a raised area topped by trees.

8. At the signpost after the bridge, take the path along the shore, ignoring the path to *Torver*. Bear right at the wire fence and go through the gate on the left following the path back to the shore and through a second gate. Walk on past the jetty and boathouse, through another gate, and into *Torver Commons*. The gravel path winds through the woods along the lakeside.

9. After the Torver Jetty on the left (Coniston Launch Ferry), take the footpath to the right signposted to *Torver*. The path climbs gently up through the woods, then joins a walled path out of Torver Common. Continue along the path past the ruins of an old stone cottage. Go through the gate and onto a wider path, which leads you past Bracken Brow Farm.

10. Cross straight over the tarmac lane and cross the stile into the field. Cross the boggy field towards the tumbled stone wall, then through the kissing gate into the next field. Using the wooden walkways where necessary, walk up to the right hand corner of the field passing a house on the right and leave the field through a metal kissing gate. Turn right onto the road and walk the short distance back to the lay-by.

FINISH

Coniston Copper Mines

Mining for copper around the Coniston area has been taking place for hundreds of years. The Romans were certainly interested in mining for all kinds of minerals in the region but there seems to be no direct evidence of copper mining at Coniston until 1599 or thereabouts.

The Elizabethan 'Company of Mines Royal' brought over experienced German miners from the Tyrol region (Schwaz and Innsbruck). The miners began their work by following veins of ore as they outcropped on the surface and later, as workings deepened, tunnels were driven in to manage drainage and to carry out extracted ore in shoulder bags.

In the days before blasting became common practice, the ore was mined with hand tools and wedges. Rocks were split using alternate fire and water and the spoil carried to mounting heaps along tunnels shaped to take a man – narrow for the head, then broadening for the shoulders before tapering to the feet - like a coffin. Some of these tunnels can still be seen by the more intrepid students of industrial archaeology.

By the mid 1600's the German miners were working at depths of over 200ft. They were followed in succeeding years by Englishmen - first from Macclesfield and later from Cornwall, who by the end of the 18th century had taken the mines down to over 1200ft with the help of a not inconsiderable number of Irishmen. There must have been a heady mix in the pubs of the time.

Copper mining in the Coniston area came to an end in 1942.

N

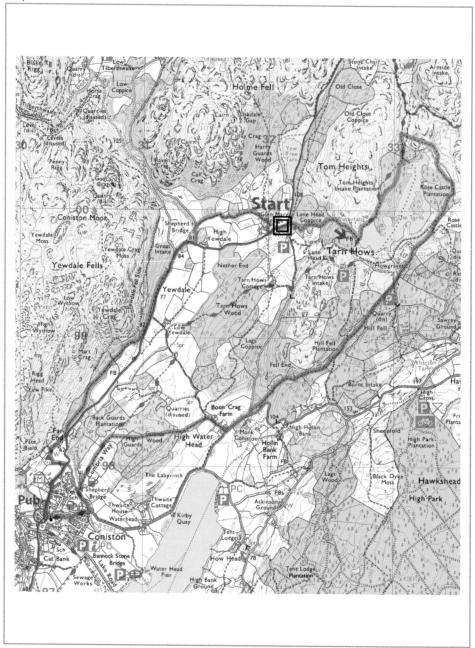

walk 6 Coniston (from Tarn Hows)

distance: **7.5 miles** | time: **3½ hours** | Start Grid Ref: **SD 321 998**

level: **moderate** | terrain: **pasture, paths and forest**

START

1. Park at the Tom Gill National Trust car park off A593. From the car park, take the footpath on the right as you face the road, into woods, signposted *Tarn Hows via Tom Gill Waterfall*. Follow the National Trust signs along the well-worn path all the way up to the top of the waterfall.

2. Go through the kissing gate at the top of the waterfall, then follow the path over the rocks and out onto a wide track at the edge of Tarn Hows. Turn left and follow the wide path around the tarn. Where the path forks, bear right. At next fork, bear right again.

3. At the northern tip of the tarn go through a gateway and continue to follow the track round to the east side of the tarn. As the path forks, take the left fork, through the gate and up the hill, signposted *Hawkshead, Old Car*

Park. Turn right at the junction to *Coniston, Hawkshead, Old Car Park.* Go through the gate into the car park at the south end of the tarn, cross the tarmac lane to the large wooden gate and join the permitted bridleway leading into the forest.

4. As path forks, take the right fork to *Coniston and Boon Crag.* Follow the broad path down the hill through the forest, and go straight ahead at the next junction, again towards *Boon Crag and Coniston.* 50 yards on, take the right fork, following the permitted bridleway. Go straight ahead on the broad gravel track (ignore the fork down to the stream on the right). At the next fork bear right, down the hill and towards the stream.

5. Cross over a small bridge and follow the stream down the hill. Cross another stream and continue to follow the wide track. At the tarmac lane, cross straight over and go through a wooden gate on to the footpath to *Coniston 1 mile.* At the end of the footpath, turn right on the road, then right again into Boon Crag Farm, following the bridle-path through the yard, past the sawmill and sheep yard. Shortly after the white cottage, turn left onto a footpath, and over a stile towards *Guards Wood and Coniston.* Follow the broad path up the hill towards the woodland. Go through the gate into Guards Wood and keep to the yellow arrows along the track over the hill.

6. At the top of the hill, pass through a gap in the drystone wall and follow the path as it begins to drop down towards a field. Go through the kissing gate and head diagonally to the left across the field to follow the path between the wall and the gorse bushes. Coniston Old Man looms ahead. Just past the gorse bushes, the path joins another wider, well-worn path coming down from the right. This is part of the *Cumbrian Way.*

Go through the gate in the wall and walk down the hill towards the Gothic Folly. Take the kissing gate at the side of the folly and follow the fenceline on the right through the field. Pass through another kissing gate in the far corner of the field beside the stream and walk along the narrow path and over the wall.

7. Turn right onto the tarmac lane and over Shepherd's Bridge. At the Primary School turn left, and pass the sports and social centre on left. At the end of this lane turn right into Coniston village, passing the church on the left (Ruskin is buried in the churchyard) and then turn right just after the shops onto Yewdale Road (A593). The Black Bull Inn is just in front of you on the opposite side of the road.

PUB - Black Bull Inn   see full pub details on page 19

8. From the pub turn left down Yewdale Road out of the village in the direction of *Ambleside* on the A593. As the road from Hawkshead comes in from the right, turn left up a little lane towards *Holly How Youth Hostel*. At the gates of the Youth Hostel continue round to the right and along the lane in front of the National Trust cottages. As the lane reaches the road again, turn left and walk a few yards down the road to a permissive bridleway on the left.

Donald Campbell

Donald Campbell's father, Sir Malcolm Campbell, chose Coniston for his 1939 attempt at the world water speed record which he achieved at a speed of 141 miles per hour. After his father's death, Donald decided to continue in the family business of speed and in 1967, during his (successful) attempt to beat 300 miles per hour, the 'Bluebird' shot into the air and sank into the depths of the lake. It was not until 2001 that divers first found 'Bluebird' and raised it from the bed of the lake and later found the remains of Campbell himself.

His body was buried in Coniston churchyard.

9. Go through the gate and follow the wide track (signposted to *Tilberthwaite*), which runs parallel to the A953 for about 1½ miles. Cross over a wide stream and look to the left to see White Gill waterfall as it cascades down Yewdale fell. At the road to Tilberthwaite on the left, follow the footpath over the junction and back along the side of the A593. In a few yards the footpath and the road diverge. Turn left onto the tarmac lane and cross over Shepherd's Bridge (another one!).

10. Take the footpath on the right after the bridge, through a kissing gate, signposted *Skelwith Bridge and Yew Tree Farm ¼ mile*. Follow the track along the drystone wall, through a kissing gate. Bear round to the right following the wall, through the gate and to the right of the rocky knoll. Continue along the track to the back of Yew Tree Farm. Turn right through the kissing gate down the hill (ignoring the yellow arrow up the hill). Walk down the track in front of the farm/B&B/Walkers Café, turn left onto the drive and walk up to the road.

11. Cross the road and go through a stile to the right, into the field in front of you. Turn left and walk up the fence-line (this avoids walking on the road back to the car park). Pass though another stile back onto the road and the car park is just to your right.

FINISH

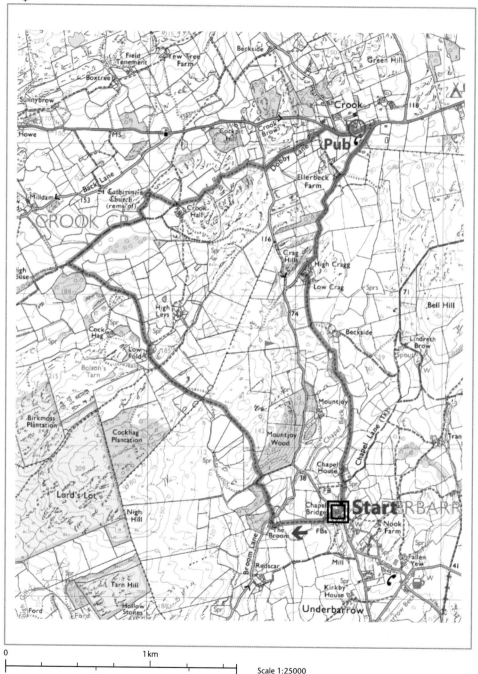

walk 7 Crook

distance: 5 miles | time: 2½ hours | Start Grid Ref: **SD 463 925**

level: **easy** | terrain: **pasture**

START

1. Park at All Saints Church in Underbarrow. This may not be possible on Sunday mornings as there are services most weeks. From the church, turn right along the road, passing the Old School House, and then take the footpath on the left after the little bridge. Walk down the path, through the gate, and into the field. Follow the yellow arrow to the right, along the beech hedge, bearing left after 20 yards or so.

2. Take the stile in the wall and cross the field, parallel to the fence-line on your left. After another stile head across the field towards a ladder stile, in front of the cottages. Pass in front of the old stone cottage, then leave the field through the wooden gate into the yard. Walk through the yard next to the cottage, then out through the wooden gate.

3. Cross straight over the road and go up the track, through the wooden gate. Walk up the

hill following the track round to the left and through the fields. Cross over the stile in the wall and then turn right, down the track. About 70 yards down the hill, take the footpath over the stile on your left. Follow this path up the steep bank (this is a tiring but short climb).

4. Over the brow of the hill, follow the wide path into the dip, and then take the left hand path, running parallel to the wall on the left. Follow the wall around to the left, do not go through the gate, but join the track going to the right up the hill. Leave the track before the wall and cross over the ladder stile to the left. Head straight up the field, going through the gap in the wall and then follow the track through the next field and over the hill.

5. At Low Fold Farm walk straight on into the yard, then cross over the stile in the wall ahead of you, to the right of Bracken Spot House. Follow the track through two fields and up over the hill. Once over the brow of the hill, continue along the track as it bears to the left. At the end of the track, bear left across the field towards a large tree stump. Shortly after the tree stump, a yellow marker directs you over to a ladder stile in the wall.

6. Cross straight over the next field and turn right in front of the slate wall to follow the track down the field to a wooden gate. Once through the gate walk straight on towards the hedge then bear right along a faint track leading towards Crook Hall Farm.

7. If you wish to visit the ruins of St Catherine's Church, take the Public Bridleway to the left before Crook Hall Farm. At the top of the field, bear right through the gates, then head over the hill. St Catherine's Church is just over the brow of the hill. From here you can rejoin the track to Crook Hall Farm by taking the footpath across the field to the right.

8. Go through the metal gate into the farmyard and bear left following the yellow marker. At the second set of yellow markers, walk straight ahead and cross over the stile in the wire fence. Bear right slightly as you cross the field to a stile in the wall. Follow the wall down the field, then walk round to the right of the rocky area in front of you. Cross over the ladder stile and then follow the hill down to a kissing gate in the drystone wall. Follow the path down the hill through the bracken, and then cross over the stile on to a tarmac lane.

9. Walk straight ahead down the lane in front of you (Dobby Lane). At the end of Dobby Lane, turn right onto Crook Road. Keep to the verge for a few yards then cross the road to use the pavement on the other side. A few hundred yards up the road is the Sun Inn.

PUB - Sun Inn
see full pub details on page 20

10. From the pub, turn left along the road and then turn right, down the lane signposted *Beckside Golf Course and Underbarrow.* Follow this lane for ¹/₂ *mile.* Shortly after the first houses on the left, High Cragg, a footpath takes you down the drive of Low Cragg. Walk through the yard and through a kissing gate that opens into pasture. Follow the wall on the left and go

through the stile in the wall. Walk parallel to the wall on the left, up to a gateway in the next wall. Continue though the field, still following the wall. After the next stile, cross over the lane and follow the sign to Underbarrow church. Follow the yellow markers through the copse of trees/bushes towards the stream, then cross over a stile in the fence and over a small wooden bridge into open pasture.

11. Bear right in the field and follow the course of Chapel Beck. Go through the kissing gate and follow the wall to your right, cross through the gate way and then walk with the wall to your left. Follow yellow markers into the next field and walk parallel to the crumbled wall towards the cottages. Go through the stile between the cottages and follow the lane down to the church.

FINISH

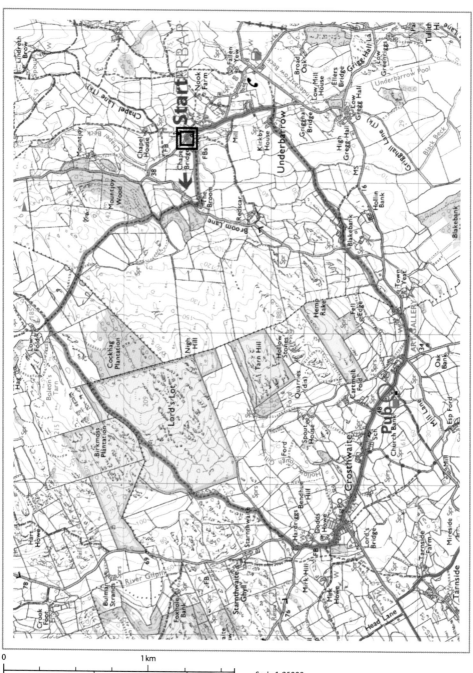

Scale 1:25000

0   1km

0   1 mile

walk 8 Crosthwaite

distance: 5 miles | time: 2½ hours | Start Grid Ref: SD 443 925

level: easy | terrain: pasture

START

Note: The starting point and first mile or so of this walk are identical to Walk 7, but the instructions are repeated here, for the sake of clarity.

1. Park at All Saints Church in Underbarrow. This may not be possible on Sunday mornings as there are services most weeks. From the church, turn right on the road, walk past the Old School House, and then take the footpath on the left after the little bridge. Go down the path, then through the gate in to the field. Follow the yellow arrow to the right, along the beech hedge, bearing left after 20 yards or so.

2. Take the stile in the wall and walk across the field, parallel to the fence-line on your left. Cross over the next stile, and then head across the field to the ladder stile and follow the path in front of the cottages, then through the wooden gate into the yard. Cross the yard next to the cottage and out through the wooden gate.

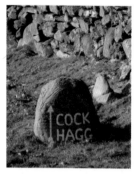

3. Cross the tarmac road and go up the track, through the wooden gate. Walk up the hill following the track round to the left, along the wall, across the stream, and up through the fields. Cross over the stile in the wall and then turn right, down the track. About 70 yards down the hill, take the footpath over the stile on your left. Follow this path up the steep bank (this is a tiring but short climb).

4. Over the brow of the hill, follow the wide path into the dip, and then take the left hand path, running parallel to the wall on the left. Follow the wall around to the left, do not go through the gate but join the track going to the right up the hill. Leave the track before the wall and cross using the ladder stile to the left of the holly tree. Head straight up the field, going through the gap in the wall and then follow the track through the next field and over the hill.

5. As you reach the signs for Low Fold, turn left and follow the footpath sign for *Crosthwaite (2 miles)* along the gravel track. A few yards down this track, before Cock Hagg, leave the track to the left and cross over the ladder stile in the wall. Head straight across the field between the two grassy mounds. At the far side, take the stile in the fence, to the left of the wall. Follow this narrow path through the gorse bushes. This path opens out and then drops down the far side of the hill through bracken.

6. Cross over the wooden stile in the fence, then bear half left, following the track up and over the hill to meet a wooden gate. Turn right in front of the gate and follow the fence-line down the hill until the fence becomes a wall. Turn left through the metal gate and turn right down the tree-lined track.

7. At the tarmac lane, turn left and into Crosthwaite. At the T-junction turn left and follow the tarmac road through the village to the church at the far end. The Punch Bowl Inn is situated next to the church just off the main road.

PUB - The Punch Bowl

see full pub details on page 21

8. From the pub turn right and follow the road out of the village. As you get to the Smithy (iron-work samples on the roadside), turn left up a tarmac lane, signposted *Public Footpath*. Walk up the hill, passing the cottages and onto the track. A short way along the

track, a yellow arrow shows the footpath off to the right, over a stile into the field. Follow the track through the middle of the field, and then go through the gate in the wall. Turn left onto the tarmac lane.

9. At High Blakebank, turn right, down the tarmac lane. On reaching Middle Blakebank follow the yellow arrow straight ahead, then at the end of the cottages, bear left in front of the white cottage and walk down the lawn to a wooden gate. Go through the gate and into the field taking the path on the ridge following a line of mature hawthorn trees and remnants of a wall. At the far side of the field, the walls on either side narrow to create a funnel shape. Walk straight down between the two walls, then at the beck go over the stile in the wall on the left.

10. Follow the wall on your right across this field, then cross over the stile and follow the yellow arrow into the next field. Head towards the green barn, round the bank to the left and go through the gate to the left of the barn into the yard. Walk down through the farmyard and at the first house turn right, then left between the two houses and right onto the driveway. Follow the driveway up to the road and turn left. Walk along the road into Underbarrow Village, and at the T-junction turn left. Keep to the road back to the church.

FINISH

N

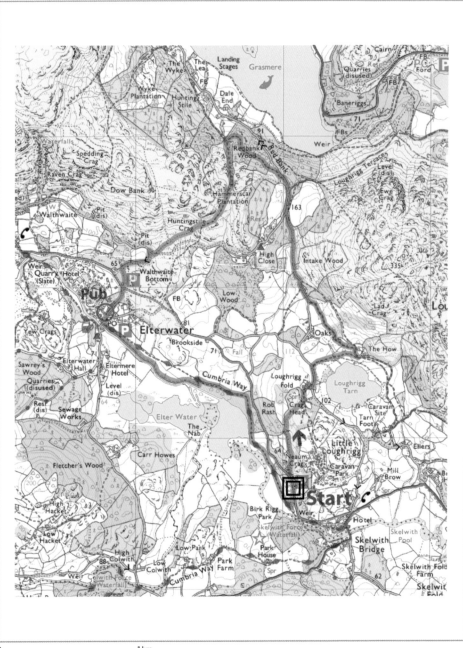

0   1km

0   1 mile

Scale 1:25000

walk 9 Elterwater

distance: 4.5 miles | time: 2½ hours | Start Grid Ref: NY 340 036

level: easy | terrain: paths

START

1. Park in Silverthwaite National Trust car park, Skelwith Bridge. From the car park take the footpath to the right of the entrance (facing the road) following the white arrows. This will lead you through a kissing gate. Follow the narrow path as it climbs the hill and winds through a young plantation of trees. As the path begins to descend towards Loughrigg Tarn, bear left towards the white cottage, then bear left again to join a wider track.

2. At the tarmac lane turn left and continue for 150 yards to a footpath over a stile on the right hand side. Loughrigg Tarn is to your right. Head straight across the field to a ladder stile over a wall, then follow the path up the hill towards the cottage. Leave the field through the wooden gate and turn left down the lane. Ahead, in the distance, you can see the Langdale Pikes.

3. Continue to the end of the dirt lane, pass through the kissing gate and turn right onto a tarmac road. Follow the road for about ½ a mile. As the road begins to descend towards Rydal, take a footpath on the left to *Grasmere*. Continue along the terrace, enjoying views of Rydal Water to your right, to a metal gate into Redbank Wood. Follow

the path through the woodland, then pass through the wooden gate and turn left towards *Elterwater and Langdale*. Go through the second gate and follow the track along the stone wall up the hill.

4. At the top of the hill (Hunting Stile Cragg), go through the wooden gate and walk along the path over the brow of the hill, dropping down towards Elterwater. Follow the widest and most well defined path down the hill towards Elterwater, bearing right as the path forks. As you reach the lane, turn right and continue down the hill. At the main road, cross over and go up the lane in to Elterwater. As you reach the Post Office, turn right and the Britannia Inn is straight ahead.

PUB - Britannia Inn
see full pub details on page 22

5. From the pub, walk across the road to the car park to the right of the Bowling Club. Follow the footpath from the car park, through the gate and join the broad gravel path at the side of the river. Continue along this path for about 1$\frac{1}{2}$ miles as it follows the river to the edge of Elterwater. Pass through a

wooden gate into open pasture, continuing to follow the broad path. Half way through the pasture, bear left. This gravel path leads to a little wooden gate, over a bridge and up through the trees towards the road. Cross the road and back to the car park.

FINISH

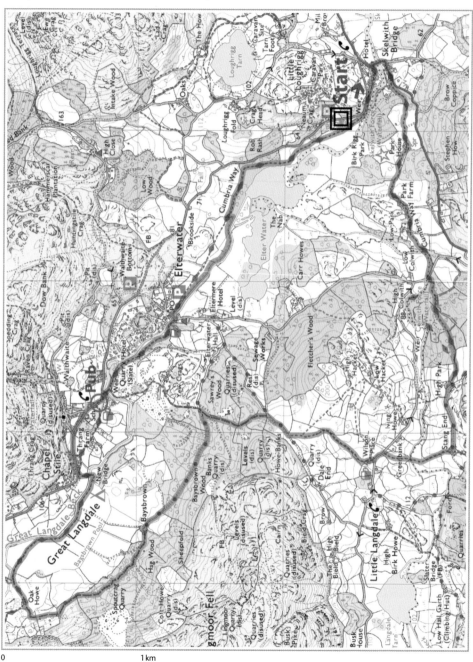

0   1 km

0   1 mile

Scale 1:25000

walk 10 Elterwater (Chapel Stile)

distance: **7.6 miles** | time: **4 hours** | Start Grid Ref: **NY 340 036**

level: **moderate** | terrain: **pasture, woodlands and paths**

START

1. Park at Silverthwaite National Trust car park on the B5343, about ¹/₂ mile from Skelwith Bridge. Cross the road and take the footpath into the woods, signposted *Langdale and Elterwater*. On meeting the main path from Elterwater, turn left, following the course of the river.

2. Continue on this path as it passes Skelwith Force waterfall (with viewing platform) until you reach the Kirkstone Quarries slate yard. Go through the yard, to emerge at Skelwith bridge itself, and turn right to follow the A593 over the bridge. Follow the road for 150 yards or so as it bends sharp right until you reach Crag Hill cottage on the right. Take the footpath into Bridge How Coppice, signposted *Colwith Bridge*. The path here is part of the *Cumbria Way* and is well marked for ¹/₂ a mile, to Park Farm and Tiplog.

3. After Park House, go through two metal kissing gates, following the yellow arrows signposted to *Colwith*, and out into a field. Go through the large wooden gate, along a broad path and follow the yellow arrows towards *Elterwater and Colwith*.

4. At Elterwater Park (Country Guest House), go through the wooden gate and bear left through the yard. At the tarmac drive, go straight on, following the yellow arrow to the right of the trees, down the path and over a stile into a field. Follow the rocky path to the left and climb the stile in the wall to join a narrow fenced path. Go through the gate at the end, then head straight across to a metal kissing gate which leads you into a field where the path snakes before you.

5. Cross over the wooden stile and follow the steps down towards the river. Climb another stile and turn right onto a tarmac lane. After 100 yards or so, take the footpath on the left before the bridge, signposted *High Park ¹/₂ mile*, over two stiles into the woods. Immediately after the second stile, take the right hand path towards *Colwith Force Waterfall*.

6. Where the path forks, the right hand fork is a short detour to Colwith Force Waterfall. Returning to the main path, continue up the track (the left fork) along the side of a wire fence. At the top of the hill, with Colwith Force on your right, follow the main path to the left, through the trees. Follow the river for a short way and then up the hill through the woodland.

7. Come out of the woodland through a kissing gate into a field, following the blue arrows. This is High Park. Follow the path around to the right, through the kissing gate into the next field and across towards the cottage. Leave the field through the gate into the farmyard following the blue arrow. Go around the building to the left and through the wooden gate onto the tarmac lane.

8. Turn right down the lane and continue until you reach the next farm, Stang End. Immediately after Stang End, as the road curves round to the right, take the footpath to the side of the cottage on your right, and go through the gate. Bear left slightly and pass through another gate onto the footpath. Continue through the next gate and head across the field towards the bridge. Cross the bridge and head to the left of the cottage to a wooden gate.

9. On the road turn left, then turn right just before Wilson Place Farm, onto the footpath following the yellow signs. Walk through the yard, then into a field through the wooden gate on the right. Follow the path up the field, over the stile in the left hand corner, then along to the path to another stile. Head through the next field to the gate in the top right corner.

10. Once on the lane, turn right and head down the hill. Just before the woodland, go through the wooden gate, then turn left onto the bridle-path into the woods. Follow the path as it winds though the woods and descends down the hill on the other side. Near the bottom of the hill, head straight over the track coming down from the left, following the blue arrow. At the tarmac lane turn left and follow this all the way to the next farm, Baysbrown Farm.

11. Go straight up through the farmyard and out through a kissing gate. Where the track forks, take the right hand fork signposted *Great Langdale and Dungeon Ghyll 2 3/4 miles.* Leave the woods and pass though the wooden gate to walk alongside the stone wall. Cross the field and go through the next wooden gate, then follow the track all the way down to the stone barn.

12. At the barn, bear right. Continue past Oak Howe Cottage, then follow the main path parallel to the river around to the right, through the fields and several gates. After the campsite turn left over the bridge and along the track up to the road. Turn right onto the road and into Chapel Stile. Carry on through the village, past the school on the right. Shortly after the village conveniences, Wainwrights Inn is on your right.

PUB - Wainwright's Inn

see full pub details on page23

13. From the pub take the bridle-path at the end of the car park. Cross over the bridge, then follow the river to the left. After a short distance, the track joins a tarmac road. Turn left down the road, which runs parallel with the river. At the end of the lane, turn left over the bridge, towards Elterwater village.

14. Shortly after the bridge, turn right into the car park behind the Bowling Club. Take the footpath through the gate and along the river. This path follows the river for around $1/2$ mile before it flows into Elterwater. Continue into the woods then out through a gate into park land.

15. Follow the gravel path through the park land, then turn left onto a narrower path up towards the road. Go through the gate and over the stream, then head up the bank to the road. Cross the road and you are back at Silverthwiate Car Park.

FINISH

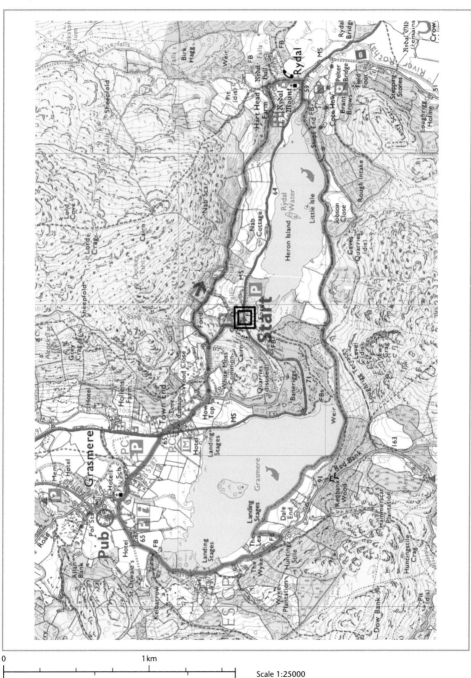

walk 11 Grasmere

distance: 5 miles | time: 2½ hours | Start Grid Ref: NY 349 065

level: easy | terrain: clear tracks, lakeside paths

START

1. Park at White Moss Common Quarry car park, off the A591 between Rydal and Grasmere. At the Rydal end of the car park, take the path that runs parallel to the road. Turn left after a few yards to join a wide rocky bridle-path. After a short climb, turn right onto a tarmac lane. After the last cottage, the tarmac lane turns into a wide rocky track.

2. At Brockstone the path narrows; pass over the small bridge and up the track though the gate. At one point the path splits, but both tracks come back to the same point and continue out of the gate in the drystone wall. Go through the next gate and over the stream; to your right you can see down to Rydal Water.

3. Leave the fields and go through a wooden gate to join a walled track. At the houses, pass through the gate and

89

continue towards the tarmac lane. Turn right at the lane, down the hill towards Rydal village and past Rydal Mount (the former home of William Wordsworth) and the church on the right.

4. At the main road, cross over carefully and turn right to walk along the pavement. A few yards down the road, take the footpath on your left, opposite the Badger Bar. Cross the footbridge and over the stile, then, as the path forks, bear right to follow the path along the edge of Rydal Water. Go through the metal kissing gate, into Rydal woods. After the second kissing gate out of the woods, take the right hand path to walk along Rydal Water shore.

Dove Cottage

Wordsworth and his sister Dorothy moved into Dove Cottage just before Christmas in 1799. It was their home until 1808 and much of Wordsworth's best work was written here. It was here too that Dorothy wrote her journals that so vividly illustrate the daily life of the poet and his family.

Dove Cottage was probably built in the very early part of the 17th century and was listed as an inn, the 'Dove and Olive', in 1617. It was a pub until 1793 and then became a house available to rent when William spotted it during a walking tour with his friend Coleridge in 1799.

It was a house of 'plain living and high thinking' and they led a very frugal existence – Sir Walter Scott recalled that they ate three meals a day, two of which were porridge. The high thinking must have been disrupted somewhat after William married Mary Hutchinson in 1802 and over a period of four years three children were born here. By 1808 the house was too small for a growing family and they moved to Allan Bank in Grasmere. Dove Cottage then became the home of a young friend of the Wordsworths, the poet, Thomas De Quincey.

5. As the path bears left, away from the lake, it begins to climb the hill steadily. At the brow of the hill, take the footpath (right fork, following the yellow arrow) down the hill towards Grasmere. At the weir, bear left on the track to drop down to the lake shore (ignore the path over the bridge to your right). Pass through the gate at the edge of the lake and follow the path closest to the shore. Continue along this track to a stone boathouse, where the path turns a right angle to the left, away from the lake. Pass through the gate in the wall (or climb the short flight of step) and turn right down the tarmac lane.

6. Follow the lane all the way to Grasmere village. As you enter Grasmere, Tweedies Bar is on your left hand side (turn down the lane, on the left before the grounds of the bar/hotel, for the entrance).

PUB - Tweedies Bar
see full pub details on page 24

7. From the pub, turn left and then left again, towards the church, (William Wordsworth and his family are buried in the churchyard). Turn right at the church and continue out of the village, down the road. At the roundabout with the A591, cross over the road, turning right, then immediately left, up the lane towards Dove Cottage. On your left is the Wordsworth Museum and Dove Cottage.

8. Continue up the lane, round to the left. At Hill Top Farm, as the road bears round to the right, take the lane to your left up the hill, following the signs for *Rydal*. Keep to the lane, past the houses, then as the lane forks, take the right hand fork down the hill onto a bridle-path to White Moss. This rocky track leads you back to the car park.

FINISH

N

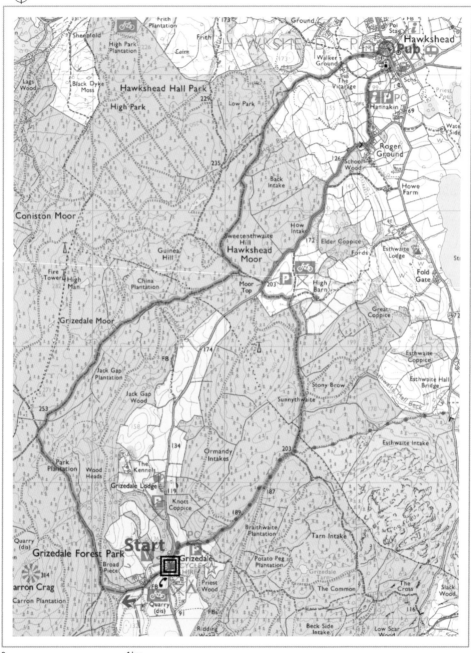

walk 12 Hawkshead (via Grizedale)

distance: 6.7 miles | time: 3½ hours | Start Grid Ref: SD 336 943

level: moderate | terrain: forest tracks

START

1. Park at Grizedale Forest Park Car Park. From the Visitors Centre and Shop, follow the red markers past the Mountain Bike hire shop, round to the left and then to the tarmac lane after the workshops. Turn right on the lane and walk up beyond the farm. As the road bends round to the right just after the farm, take the track straight up into the trees, following the red, green and yellow footpath markers. Take the footpath on the right, up the steps and continue to follow it up the hill.

2. At the wide dirt road, turn right. A short way along the road, take the left fork onto the bridleway, following the red and green markers. At the next fork, go straight on, leaving the red and green markers. At the dirt road, turn right again, following the yellow public footpath marker. Turn right at the next T-junction, then, as the path forks again, turn right.

3. After ¼ mile, take the right hand fork down the hill. As you reach a broad dirt road coming down from the right, bear left. After 25 yards, take the bridle-path on the left, following the blue arrow. As you meet the track coming in from the left, turn right, then turn left, onto the dirt road. On your right is a small tarn with a Grizedale sculpture – The Pinnacles (74).

4. A short distance down the track, take the left hand fork, following the blue cycle path arrow. As the track forks in three directions, take the right hand fork. Continue over the brow of the hill, and, as you begin to descend, you can see Lake Windermere in the distance. A short way down the hill, as you reach the clearing with fields to your right, take the Permissive Bridleway on the right. As the narrow path forks, follow the blue arrow to the left. Go through the small kissing gate and continue down the hill.

5. Walk behind the cottages and past Walker Ground B&B, then, at the tarmac lane, turn left, signposted to *Hawkshead Village*. At the white cottages the lane forks, take the right hand fork and the Kings Arms Hotel is a short way down the narrow lane to your left. Continue around the outside of the hotel to find the front entrance in The Square.

PUB - King's Arms Hotel
see full pub details on page 25

6. From the front entrance to the hotel, turn left out of the square, to the main shopping area of Hawkshead. Follow the road around to the right, then, as you reach the public toilets (in front of Tourist Information Centre), turn right, through the large metal gate, up to the school and church. Walk on, past

the school museum (school attended by Wordsworth), and into the churchyard. Follow the path straight on through the yard and out of a gate in the top left hand corner. Pass through a wooden gate, then turn left towards Roger Ground. Go through the kissing gate and follow the path all the way to the houses at Roger Ground.

7. At the tarmac lane, turn right up the hill. Follow this lane for around 1 mile, towards Grizedale Forest. As you reach the top of the hill, at Moor Top Forestry Commission Car Park, turn left onto a footpath towards *High Barn and Esthwaite Water*. At the wooden signpost, turn right off the main track, towards *Grizedale Centre and The Fox*. Follow the yellow markers over the boggy area using the wooden walkway. Go through the gate in the deer fencing and follow the path into the forest.

8. At the clearing, turn left onto the wide dirt road. As the track bends sharply to the left, take the footpath straight ahead, off the main track, following the yellow arrow. Follow the narrow path through the gate and into the forest. As you reach the clearing on the other side of the forest, turn right onto the dirt road. On your right now is sculpture number 75, The Fox.

9. Continue down the dirt road, then bear right at the T-junction. One hundred yards or so down the road, turn left down a rocky track. The track leads you down the hill and brings you out across the road from the visitors centre.

FINISH

N

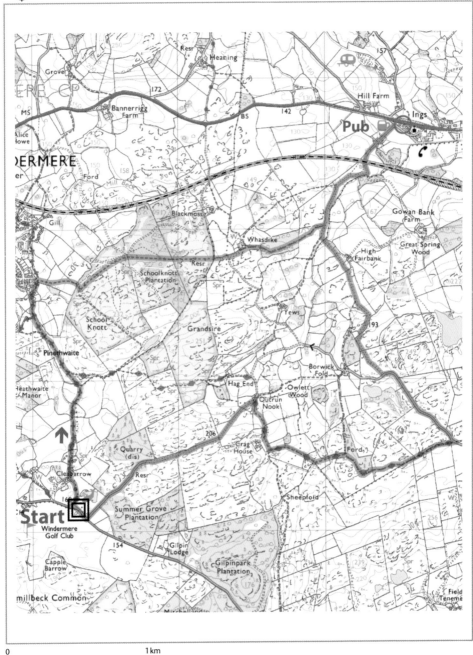

0   1 km

Scale 1:25000

0   1 mile

walk 13 Ings

distance: 6 miles | time: 2½ hours | Start Grid Ref: SD 422 961

level: easy | terrain: pasture

START

1. Park in the lay-by opposite the golf course on the B5284, between Crook and Bowness-on-Windermere, by the signs for the *Dales Way*. Turn up the tarmac lane, following the red arrow, for a public byway to the *Dales Way*. Continue past the cottages until the tarmac lane becomes a gravel track. Follow the track for around ¾ mile, walking straight on at the right turn for the *Dales Way*, continuing through several gates until you reach a tarmac lane. Bear right here, down the hill and continue past the cottages.

2. Go through the tall wooden gate, then turn right to join the footpath to *School Knott*. After the next wooden gate, bear left to follow the faint track that runs almost parallel to the wall on your left. A short diversion to the top of School Knott, to your right, is well worth the short climb, to enjoy wonderful views of Lake Windermere.

3. After a short distance a yellow marker shows your way over to a kissing gate into School Knott Plantation. Follow the track through the plantation and at the yellow arrow, go straight ahead, through the kissing gate and out of the plantation, into the field.

4. Head straight across the field towards the tarmac lane, on the far side, past the low building with the corrugated iron roof. At the lane turn right and pass through the black and white metal gate. As the lane forks, bear left to Wasdike Farm. Turn right in front of the gateway to follow the bridleway (blue arrow) along the wall towards the woodland.

5. Pass through the gate and follow the track through the woods. Once out of the woods, head across the field (slightly to the left) following the blue arrow.

6. As you reach the tarmac lane, turn left and follow this lane all the way to Ings village. Turn right at the end of the lane and the Watermill Inn is just in front of you.

PUB - The Watermill Inn
see full pub details on page 26

7. From the pub, retrace your steps back down the lane and carry on past the bridle-path where you originally joined the lane. Continue up the gated lane, past High Fairbank and over the hill. At the lane end, cross over the cattle grid and turn left

8. After ¹/₄ mile turn right onto a walled bridleway, signposted for the *Dales Way*. At the end of the track, go through a gate on your right and bear left following the faint track through the field. In the second field, bear right, following the marker posts.

9. After the woodland on your right, walk straight on to join a footpath, as the bridleway bears right around the edge of the wood. Go through the kissing gate and follow the yellow markers across the field, around the gorse bushes to your right. Cross over the stile and follow the track up the hill towards the farm. Pass through the gate at the farm buildings and continue up the track with the farm on your left, then follow the *Dales Way* markers around to the right along the wall. Pass through the wooden gate and walk down the field, bearing left slightly.

10. To the left of the house at Outrun Nook, pass through the kissing gate and turn left on to the tarmac lane. Continue along the lane, over the hill and down, towards the main road (B5284). At the main road, turn right and your car is a short distance away.

FINISH

N

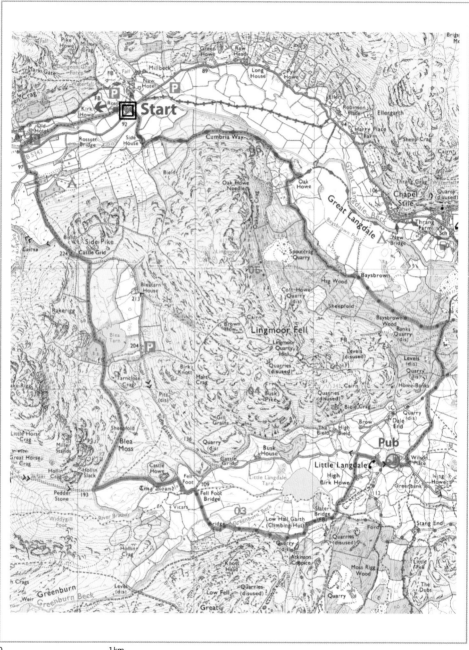

0   1 km

0   1 mile

walk 14 Little Langdale

distance: 8 miles | time: 4½ hours | Start Grid Ref: NY 294 063

level: strenuous | terrain: rocky tracks, woodland

START

1. Park in the National Trust Car park on the right, just after the New Dungeon Ghyll Hotel. Take the footpath to the right of the coach parking bay, near the entrance of the car park, through the gate and into the field. Walk across the field in front of the cottage and through the next gate, turning immediately to the right over a small bridge. Turn left into the field and follow the track along the fence-line to a stile. Climb the stile and head across the paddock to a wooden gate. Go straight on through two more fields, with Old Dungeon Ghyll Hotel to your right as you walk through the last field. Go through the gate and turn left, over a stone bridge on the tarmac lane.

2. At the junction, turn right, then a few yards down the road turn left at the post box, towards the campsite. As the lane bears right, take the footpath on the left into

the campsite. Follow the gravel path off the main tarmac drive to the right, through the trees. Walk across the paddock, through a kissing gate and up the path between the trees to a second kissing gate. Go diagonally across the field to the right, towards the copse of trees, through another kissing gate and into the wood. Follow the rocky track through the wood to the next gate.

3. The path now goes up the steep hill, parallel with the wall on the right. As the path begins to level out near the brow of the hill, there is a cattle grid in the tarmac lane to your right. Go over the ladder stile next to the cattle grid, cross the lane and walk down to the kissing gate further down the wall. Go through the gate and follow the path that leads down to Blea Tarn.

4. Go through a kissing gate into the woodland at the west side of the tarn, then, as the track forks, take the stone path out of the wood and away from the tarn, through a kissing gate. Follow the stream to your left and negotiate the large boulders carefully. Once past the rocks, the path runs alongside a drystone wall for a short way, before continuing round the hill, to the right across some boggy land. Follow the faint path and head towards the tarmac lane.

5. On the lane, turn left and head down the hill. Walk past the farm, then turn right over the stone bridge, through a gate and onto a walled footpath, which is part of the *Cumbrian Way*. Go through the next gate and follow the track around the National Trust cottage. Continue along the stoney track for roughly 1 mile.

6. At the fork in the track, take the left fork, down towards the stone cottage, High Hallgarth. Continue over the stream and through the wooden gate, walking past the cottage and onto a path with slate under foot. Continue past the other cottages, then, $1/4$ mile down the path, go through a kissing gate on the left towards *Slater's Bridge*. Cross over Slater's Bridge and walk up the hill to Birk House Farm. Go though the gate and turn left down the farm track. At the end of the track, turn right onto the lane and follow it down the hill and round the corner to the Three Shires Inn.

PUB - Three Shires Inn
see full pub details on page 27

7. From the pub turn left, continuing down the lane. At Wilson Place Farm take the footpath on your left, signposted *Elterwater*, past the cottages, and up through the yard. Go through the gate on the right and follow the path through the field along the fence. Go over the stile in the corner of the

field and then along a narrow path to a second stile leading into an open field. Follow the path across the field to the gate, then turn right on to a track heading down hill.

8. Immediately after the wooden gate, turn left onto a bridleway leading into the woods. Follow the rocky track through the woods all the way down the hill. Cross straight over the wide vehicle track that comes down from the left. At the tarmac lane turn left, following this lane all the way to Baysbrown Farm.

9. Walk straight on through the farmyard, then, as the path forks, bear right on to a narrower path, signposted *Great Langdale and Dungeon Ghyll 2 3/4 miles*. Continue along the path until you reach a large stone barn.

10. At the Barn (Oak Howe) turn left onto a footpath, following the yellow arrows. Continue through two kissing gates, and at the second gate you can see the New Dungeon Ghyll car park, across the valley to your right. After the second gate follow the stone path down the hill and through the gate towards the farm. Cross over the bridge and go through another gate to the right of the stone buildings. Follow the yellow markers down the driveway back to the road. Cross over the road to get back to the car park.

FINISH

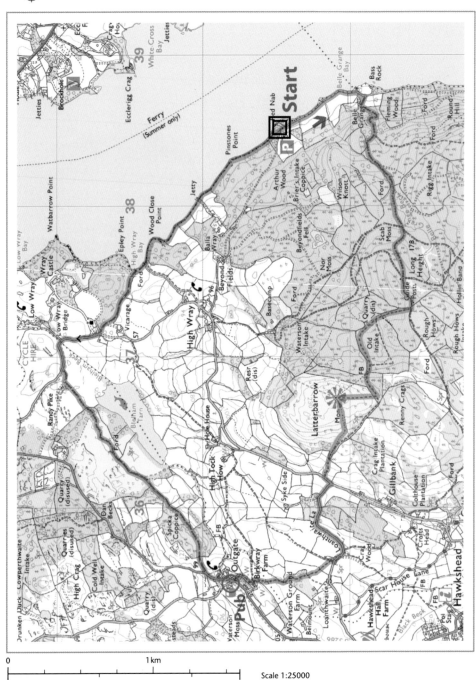

walk 15 Outgate

distance: 7 miles | time: 3½ hours | Start Grid Ref: SD 384 994

level: moderate | terrain: forest tracks and pasture

START

1. Park at the National Trust car park at Red Nab next to Lake Windermere near Wray Castle (free parking). From the car park, walk down the track with the lake on your left hand side, towards Belle Grange. Immediately after Belle Grange (the large white house), turn right onto the bridle-path to *Latterbarrow, Hawkshead and Near Sawrey*, heading up the hill into the woods.

2. As you reach the small clearing with the stone ford on your left, continue straight ahead up the rocky track, signposted *Hawkshead via Guideposts*. At the wide track that crosses your path (bridle-path to *High Wray*), go straight over then bear right onto the path, signposted *Hawkshead via Guideposts*. Cross straight over the next track and continue on the bridle-path towards Hawkshead.

3. After a short distance, turn right in front of a wooden gate onto a footpath, following the yellow arrow towards Latterbarrow. The rocky path drops steeply down the hill, bearing left at the bottom of the hill, then climbs a steep bank. Turn right at the top of the bank and follow the path until it becomes a wide track leading you through mature conifers. Follow this track for around ¼ mile, as it winds through the forest.

4. As you reach the edge of the wood, cross over the wooden stile, then take the path to the right, to the summit of Latterbarrow. From the summit you can enjoy panoramic views of the Lakeland Hills. As you reach the cairn, Hawkshead village is away to your left. Take the path downhill in the direction of Hawkshead. Follow the path as it descends the side of Latterbarrow, bearing right as you reach the trees. Continue along the path into the field and down towards the wooden gate.

5. Go through the gate and turn left down the tarmac lane. After about 60 yards, turn right down a narrow lane. Continue along this lane to High Loanthwaite Farm B&B. Shortly after the farmhouse, turn right through a wooden gate. After a few yards, cross over the stile on the left onto the footpath to Outgate. Cross the field and climb the stile into the second field, following the yellow arrow across to the trees. Follow the path through the trees, then cross over another stile and follow the yellow arrow to the right, in the direction of the houses. Pass through another kissing gate, bear right, then follow the paddock round to the left. Pass through a metal kissing gate, which brings you to the back of the Outgate Inn.

PUB - Outgate Inn
see full pub details on page 28

Belle Isle and The Mutiny on the Bounty

In 1774 the uncompleted Round House on the largest island on Windermere was bought by Isabella Curwen after whom the name 'Belle Isle' was coined.

John Christian, Isabella's husband, was the cousin of Fletcher Christian the infamous mutineer. Family rumour has it that Fletcher returned to England from Pitcairn Island and hid at Belle Isle. Certainly John Curwen, as he was known after his marriage, attempted to save the family's reputation by blackening that of Capt Bligh.

The poet Wordsworth also assisted in collecting evidence to defend the mutineer against Bligh's accusations. Fletcher Christian had seized the Bounty after the crew had suffered weeks of vicious insults by William Bligh. The Captain and his loyal crewmen were cast off in an open boat, with food and water but without navigational instruments.

After his return to England and a court martial Bligh was exonerated for the loss of his ship and became a great national hero. Something of the story of Fletcher Christian has apparently been fictionalised in Coleridge's poem ' The Rime of the Ancient Mariner'.

John Curwen became a Whig MP, agricultural pioneer and early welfare reformer when he instituted a compulsory sickness and unemployment benefit scheme for his workers. His descendants continued to live on Belle Isle until 1993.

6. From the entrance to the pub, turn right and walk up the road towards *Ambleside* (there is no pavement, so be aware of traffic). A 100 yards past the last house in the village, turn right onto a rocky bridle-path. Follow this track down the hill, then through the fields with Blelham Tarn off to your right and follow the signpost to *Low Wray and Wray Castle*. After a short distance, cross over a shallow ford using the large stepping-stones and continue along the clear track.

7. As you reach the metal gate at the road, turn right and walk along the permitted path following the hedge to avoid walking along the busy road. At the corner of the field, pass through the kissing gate and turn right onto the road, being careful of traffic. Shortly after the Dower House and Wray Castle College, turn left down the bridle-path and follow the track through the woodland and down towards Lake Windermere. As you reach the lake, continue to follow the track along the shore. This path takes you directly back to Red Nab car park ($1^1/_2$ miles).

FINISH

N

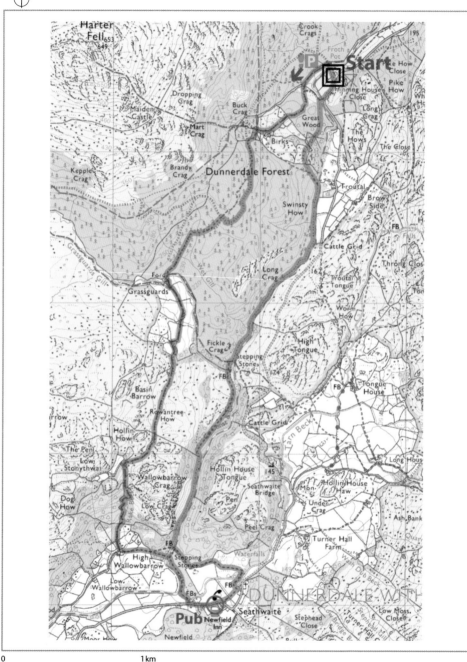

0   1km

0   1 mile

Scale 1:25000

walk 16 Seathwaite

distance: 6 miles | time: 4 hours | Start Grid Ref: SD 235 995

level: moderate | terrain: forest tracks and rocky paths

START

1. Park at Birk Bridge Forestry Commission Car Park, North of Seathwaite in Dunnerdale Forest. From the car park, cross over the bridge, then take the bridle-path (blue arrow) off to the left, over some boggy ground, to walk alongside the river. Follow the path round the fence-line on your right, cross over the stream, then up, towards the woods through the gap in the wall. Walk straight ahead as the path forks onto a wider cobbled track coming in from the left. Follow the track through the woods, taking the right fork up the hill through the wooden gate.

2. Follow the grassy path up through another gate and turn right before the buildings of Birks Field Study Centre. Go through the left hand gate then turn immediately left up a path to join a vehicular track coming in from the right. Turn left again onto the track and walk up the hill.

3. Over the brow of the hill you will reach a cleared area. Take the path on the left, through the cleared forest to join a wider forest track. Turn left at the track and walk down the hill. At the ford, cross over the bridge and pass through the gate into the farmyard of Grassguards Farm. Walk straight through the yard and out of another gate to join a grassy bridle-path.

4. After the derelict farm buildings the clear track passes through a gateway and then bends left to run between two stone walls to another gate, next to a ladder stile. Pass through the tall gates and through the area of newly planted native trees. As you round Wallerbarrow Cragg, turn left at Stoneythwaite Farm, following the blue arrows. The track now descends steeply to the south of Wallerbarrow Cragg.

5. At the bottom of the track, pass through the gates into the farmyard and follow the footpath signs round to a gate on the left (Signposted *Seathwaite*). Cross the paddock and through the gate into the next field. Follow the path across the field, towards the woods. Go through the gate and take the right-hand footpath, towards the river. Cross the River Duddon, using the stepping-stones or the bridge a little further upstream. Turn right to follow the river downstream. Cross over the bridge, pass through the gate and out of the woods. At the tarmac lane, turn left. A few hundred yards up the lane you will find the Newfields Inn.

PUB - Newfield Inn   see full pub details on page 29

6. From the pub, cross over the road, bearing slightly left and take the footpath between the cottage and the barn. Head across the field, towards the signpost to *Stepping-Stones and Memorial Bridge*. Cross over the small bridge and follow the track through the woodland. Cross back over the River Duddon by the stone Memorial Bridge and turn right to join a permissive path heading up stream.

7. The path becomes very rocky and you may have to negotiate large boulders. As you reach the highest point of the path, follow the white markers through a boggy area of ground. The path then descends, winding down into the valley to meet the river again and crossing a wooden bridge over a stream coming down from the left. As you reach the stepping-stones over the river to your right, continue straight ahead along the riverside path following the white arrow to *Birks Bridge*.

8. Cross over the beck, with the waterfall to your left, and continue along the path through a wood of coppiced Beech trees, followed by a thick conifer plantation. Shortly after the thick forest, carry straight on along the river, then turn left up a faint path, ignoring the bridge to your right.

9. As the path levels slightly entering a clearing, turn right up over the rocky knoll, and pass between the large rocks. This is a permissive footpath that takes a shortcut away from the yellow markers. At the top, keep walking straight ahead, over the large boulder and into woodland. Cross the stile and follow the white markers through the woods. At the stone bridge, cross the river and then turn left, following the path along the river, until you reach Birks Bridge and the car park.

FINISH

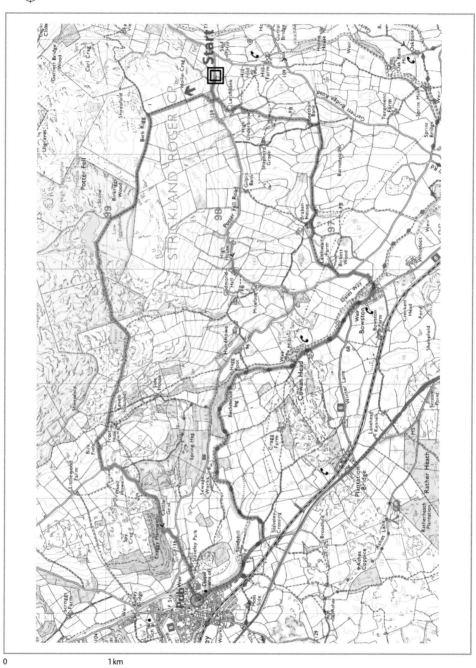

0   1 km

0   1 mile

118

walk 17 Staveley

distance: 8 miles | time: 4 hours | Start Grid Ref: SD 516 980

level: moderate | terrain: pasture and open fell

START

1. Park in a lay-by on Potter Fell Road (at the eastern end, close to the phone box), not in a passing place or blocking any gateways. Follow the lane up the hill and take the first footpath on the right, through the gate and along the track around to the right. Head up the hill, then follow the drystone wall on your right. Go through the gate, located at the top right hand corner of the field, then turn left onto a grassy lane.

2. After ¹/₄ mile, pass through the wooden gate and continue along the track. Just before Gurnal Dubs Tarn, follow the yellow footpath marker to the left and after a short distance, follow the footpath uphill to the left, after the boat house. Cross over the ladder stile, then follow the widest track down the hill, heading towards Potter Tarn.

3. Cross the stream, climb the stile and follow the path to the left - Potter Tarn is to your right. Cross over the ladder stile into the next field, then follow the yellow arrow to the right of the small hill. The path begins to descend, and soon leads you through a metal gate in the wall. Bear right after the gate, then pass through the gap in the wall and take the most worn track off to the left.

4. As you reach the wide track in front of the wall, turn right, then go through the metal gate in the wall just before the *no right of way* sign. Follow the wall straight down the field, through the gateway next to the woods and then round the edge of the field, keeping the stream on your left hand side.

Go through the wooden gate, over the stream, and follow the shady lane to the farm cottage (Birk Field). Pass through the wooden gate at the end of the cottage and walk through the yard up to the right, past the barn, then leave the yard through a metal gate along the driveway.

5. As you reach the tarmac lane, turn left and follow this gated lane through the fields and past the woodland for around ³/₄ mile. At the T-junction, turn right up the shady lane, then in 50 yards or so, take the footpath on the left through the gate. Pass through the kissing gate at the end of the paddock, then through the metal kissing gate just ahead and to the right, which leads you down a narrow path. At the river, turn right along the path, then cross over the bridge to the left.

6. At the end of this path (churchyard on left, Duke William Pub on right), turn left and walk along the pavement at the side of the road. Walk through Staveley village, and over the bridge, the Eagle & Child is ahead of you on the right, the beer garden to the left.

PUB - Eagle & Child
see full pub details on page 30

7. From the pub, turn right and walk out of the village along the pavement, following the river down stream. Just before you reach the level crossing, turn left through a wooden gate to join the *Dales Way* footpath. A short way down the track, turn left through a kissing gate, following the signs for the *Dales Way*. Walk through the field, following the path around the corner of the drystone wall. Pass through the kissing gate, turn right onto the track, through the next kissing gate and follow the track alongside the river. Stay on the path along the river for around 2 miles as you pass through several fields and climb the stiles.

8. When you reach Cowan Head (a large modern development, behind the weir in the river) go through the metal gate and follow the tarmac drive in front of the white cottages. As the driveway bends to the right, walk straight ahead onto the shady track, following the river on your left hand side. Follow the path between the cottages, then at the end of the path, turn left on to the road. Walk down into the village of Bowston. At the red post-box, turn left and cross over the bridge, out of the village.

Staveley Mill Yard

Staveley Mill Yard began its life in bobbin manufacture – the bobbins taken south for use in Lancashire cotton mills. In recent years it has metamorphosed into an eclectic mix of dynamic enterprises including a micro-brewery (Hawkshead), a Cookery School (Lucy's of Ambleside) and, wait for it, the only whisky distillery south of the border (Lakeland Distillers Ltd). The first Lakeland Single Malt should be in production by summer 2007 with the first 50 barrels on offer to those with no liquidity problems, at £5000 each. The Mill Yard is well worth a visit.

It started out as Chadwick Mill in 1841 using local coppiced timber to make the bobbins with machinery powered by the waters of the River Kent, England's fastest flowing river. Owned by Benjamin Turton, a member of a textile manufacturing family, almost all of the production went to one of the family's spinning mills at Eagley Bank near Bolton.

The Mill was sold in 1897 and shortly afterwards became 'The Staveley Wood Turning Co. Ltd', eventually coming into the hands of the Brockbank family, some of whom had operated the bobbin machinery in years gone by. As demand declined in the cotton spinning industry, production moved successfully from bobbins to tool handles and at its height the mill probably employed about 200 people. Conditions were hard as the buildings were not enclosed and winter working sometimes meant using dangerous machinery in flurries of snow. Losing fingers was commonplace.

The Mill Yard remains to this day under the control of the Brockbanks who continue to develop it whilst preserving some of its history. The vertical pillars of the old coppice drying sheds can still be seen incorporated into the walls of some of the small business units on the site and some of the power transmission line shafting from the old water wheel remains on view upstairs in Wilf's Café. The River Kent is still used as a source of power as its water flows through turbines deep under the mill to produce electricity.

9. Shortly after a lane on the right, turn right down the driveway to Laithwaite Farm (footpath is not signposted). Once in the farmyard, bear left, after the open sided barn, into the field. Walk around the corner of the wall to the right and cross over the stile next to the metal gate. The footpath heads up the field, following the line of telegraph poles. In the top right hand corner of the field, climb the stile and cross over the stream. Walk straight ahead, through the gate next to the cattle grid.

10. Cross the tarmac lane and join a walled bridleway to *Beetham Bank*, bearing right at Braban House. The track takes a left hand turn and passes through a wooden gate into a field. Follow the tumbled stone buildings around to the right and join the path along the stone wall. As the wall bends round to the right, follow the clear path down across the field. The path now follows the stone wall on your left. As you reach the crumbled part of the stone wall, pass through a wooden gate into the next field (you can see Barnsdale Farm away to your right). Continue and follow the fence and wall on your right, through the fields until you join a wide farm track that drops steeply down to Beetham Bank Farm.

11. Go through the metal gate and turn left up to the farmyard. In the farmyard, pass through the gate to the right of the

white cottage, through the second gate and into the field. Walk straight across the field, then follow the hedgerow to the left to locate the stile. Cross over the stream and head up the field towards the cottage. Just to the right of the cottage, pass through a small wooden gate, then bear right down the gravel drive and out of the gate.

12. At the tarmac lane, turn left then take the footpath over the metal ladder into the field. Head across the field, towards the next farm buildings. Go through the gate in the corner of the field and farmyard. Immediately after the first of the farm buildings on the right, turn right and go through the stile in the drystone wall. Walk down the steps, then head across the field, to a stile over the wall on the far side. Turn left after the stile and walk up towards the white cottage, crossing over another stile and pass the cottage through the yard. Shortly after the gardens, take the stile in the wall on the right hand side. Head diagonally across the field, up the hill, then out of the gate and turn right down to the lay-by on Potter Fell Road.

FINISH

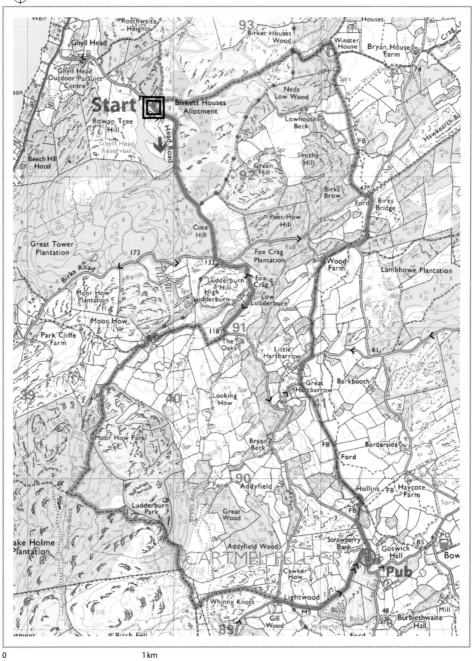

0   1km

0   1mile

Scale 1:25000

walk 18 Strawberry Bank

distance: 7.2 miles | time: 3½ hours | Start Grid Ref: SD 398 924

level: moderate | terrain: pasture and woodland

START

1. Park in the lay-by next to Ghyll Head Access Area, opposite the reservoir. Take care not to block access to the gates. Walk along the road in an easterly direction, with the reservoir on your right hand side. Continue to the road end. At the junction, turn left towards *Winster and Kendal*, and follow the lane over the hill. (Ignore the next left, down to the ford.)

2. At the bottom of the hill, as the lane bends round to the left towards the farm, turn right onto a public footpath to *Birks Road*. Go through the two metal gates and along the track through the field. Before the next gate, follow the yellow arrow to the right. Bear left at the end of the field and go over the stile next to the wooden gate. Head up the bank to the right and go through the old gateway next to the oak tree, to join a grassy track. Go through the small gate and walk into

the yard in front of the white cottage. Cross the lawn by the stepping-stones, to the left of the cottage, and join a narrow path. Go through the small gate and then over the stile in the wall to your left. Walk past the cottage on your right, then go up the steps next to the stone barn, and through the wooden gate into the field.

3. Follow the path straight ahead to a wooden gate. Go through the gate and cross the field to a ladder stile. On the other side join the track and continue to the woodland. To your right you can enjoy wonderful views across Windermere and, in the distance, the Lakeland Fells. Cross over the stile in the fence and follow the path as it winds through the woodland.

4. At a junction in the path, follow the yellow arrow up the hill to the left. Where a vehicle track goes off to the left, keep straight ahead. At the top of the hill, you reach a clearing with excellent views to the left. Follow the narrower path away from the clearing as you begin to descend through the woodland on the other side of the hill. Cross over the stile and continue through a boggy area of ground. Once past this boggy area, the narrow path leads you into a conifer plantation.

5. Turn left at the tumbled slate building. Cross over the stile in the wall into open pasture. Walk to the left of the rocky knoll, then head down the field towards the lane. Go through the wooden gate and bear right to the lane junction in front of *Lightwood Country Guest House*. Turn left at the junction and follow this lane downhill for ¹/₂ mile to the Mason's Arms.

PUB - Mason's Arms
see full pub details on page 31

6. From the pub, turn left down the lane, with views of the Winster Valley off to your right. After a short distance, turn right down a driveway, onto a public bridleway to *Hollins Farm*. Walk through the yard in front of the house, then go through the metal gate between the house and the barn. Walk straight ahead, down the walled track. Cross over the stream as you come into the field, and continue straight ahead, keeping the fence-line on your right. Go through the wooden gate and then cross the field to another gate. Follow the track across the next field and go out of the gate onto the lane. Turn right and follow the lane, down the hill.

7. A short way down the lane, take the public bridleway on the left to *Wood Farm*, up the track and through the trees. Go through the gate into the field, heading straight across to a gap in the wall and into the next field. Go through the gateway and follow the faint track across the stream and over the field to a wooden gate. Follow the fence on your left hand side, to another gate, where you join a walled grassy track. Follow the track past the stone barn, then at the T- junction, turn right.

8. Cross over the stream then bear left up to the tarmac lane, where you turn left again. At the ford turn left and cross the stream over the stone bridge. Shortly after the ford, turn right onto a public footpath. Go through the kissing gate and follow the wide track through the field. As the track begins to bend round to the left, leave the track and head straight across the field to a stile over the drystone wall. There is a fine example of a lime kiln to your left, before the wall. Go past the tumbled wall, over the stream and then bear left to a wooden gate next to the trees. Go through the gate and up the narrow green lane.

9. As you reach Winster House, turn left up the tarmac driveway, through the stone gateposts. Follow the drive round to the left, then head straight up the hill to a public footpath, along a rocky track. At the top of the track, go through the tall wooden gate and turn left, then immediately right, along a footpath through Candlestick Moss (SSSI). Continue along the path, through the moss, and back to the car park through a large wooden gate.

FINISH

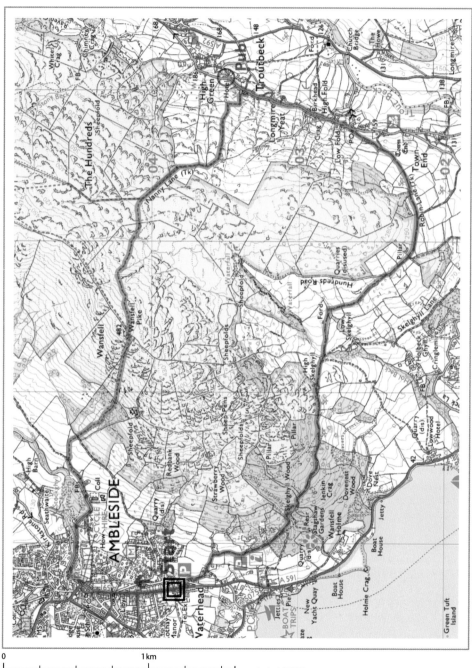

walk 19 Troutbeck (via Wansfell)

distance: 6.5 miles | time: 4 hours | Start Grid Ref: NY 376 038

level: strenuous | terrain: open fell and pasture

START

1. Park in the car park on the right, just after Hayes Garden Centre, on the A591. From the car park, turn right along the A591 into Ambleside. Turn right again, between the White Lion Inn and Natwest bank. Follow the sign for the *Waterfalls and Stockghyll Force* to the left.

2. Take the public footpath on the left to Stockghyll Force through the gate, and then follow the red arrows signs along the beck up to the waterfalls. Near the top of the falls, turn right, signposted *Revolving Gate and Wansfell*. Go through the gate and turn left up a tarmac track.

3. As the track opens up into pasture, go through the stile on the right, signposted *Troutbeck via Wansfell*. Follow the path straight on through the

field, and through the gate. Then follow the step-like path all the way up Wansfell. This is a long and tiring climb but the views are spectacular and well worth the effort.

4. At the top, follow the path to the left, up to the rocky summit of Wansfell Pike. (You may avoid the climb to the summit by taking the path to the right, then climb the style over the wall.) On the other side of the summit, take the path ahead, bearing slightly left (in a north easterly direction) and head towards the stone wall. Go through the wooden gate and follow the path in front of you, across the field. Go through the next gate and turn right down a walled track (Nanny Lane). Follow this bridle-path all the way down into Troutbeck.

5. At the road, turn left and walk a few hundred yards to the Mortal Man Inn on the left.

PUB - Mortal Man
see full pub details on page 32

6. From the pub turn left, retracing your steps along the road and through Troutbeck Village. Immediately after the post office, turn right up a walled bridle-path, (Robin Lane). As you round the hill, take the gate on the left with a faint stone sign for *Ambleside*.

7. At the gate, with the beck to your right, turn right up the tarmac track towards the farm. Walk through the farm to a wooden gate on the right, to the rear of the farmhouse. Go through the second gate and follow the path to Stockghyll Woods.

8. Go through the gate into the woods and follow the broad path, keeping to the main track that bears right around the hill at a steady descent. Soon, the path becomes a walled lane. Follow this lane past the houses to the bottom of the hill. At the end of the lane turn right and you find yourself back in the car park.

FINISH

Townend

Townend, now owned by the National Trust, is the only 'statesman' (wealthy yeoman farmer) house surviving unaltered in the Lake District today. It was built by the Browne family in the early 1600's and was occupied by succeeding generations until 1943. It is remarkable not only as a fine example of vernacular architecture, with its round chimneys, mullioned windows and lime roughcast walls, but also for the wealth of accumulated contents including many delicately carved pieces of oak furniture.

The last male member of the Browne family to live at Townend was George Browne (1834 – 1914), who seems to have taken early retirement from the family business of sheep farming to concentrate on his passion for wood carving. Many examples of his work can be seen in the house including carved chairs and cabinet work.

The house is best appreciated on a bright day as the interior is rather dark and there are no electric lights. It is open from the end of March to the end of October, Wednesday to Sunday, with a 'Mr Browne' on hand most Thursdays. See National Trust for details.

N

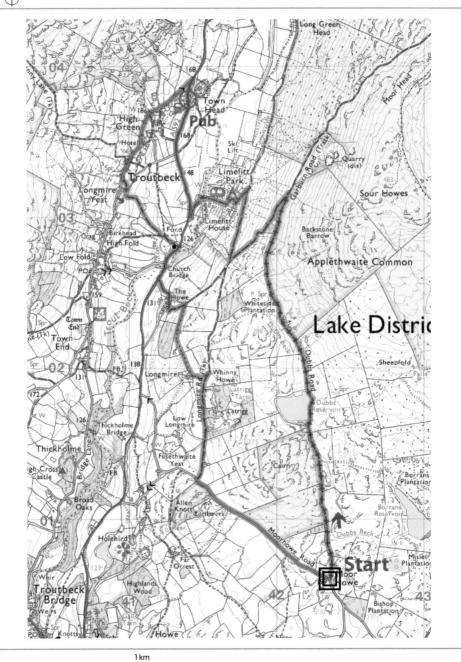

0   1 km

0   Scale 1:25000   1 mile

walk 20 Troutbeck Valley

distance: 6 miles | time: 2$\frac{1}{2}$ hours | Start Grid Ref: NY 423 005

level: moderate | terrain: rocky tracks

START

1. Park in the lay-by next to the track leading to Dubs Reservoir on the Moorhowe Road from Ings to Troutbeck (*No Through Road* sign on right hand side of road). Walk up the walled track and follow this for around 1$\frac{1}{2}$ miles, passing Dubs Reservoir along the way.

2. Shortly after a small plantation of mature conifers on the left of the track, turn left. From here you can enjoy fantastic views across the Troutbeck Valley to Wansfell, Troutbeck Tongue and High Street.

3. After $\frac{1}{4}$ mile, turn right through a wooden gate and join a bridle-path towards Limefit Caravan Park. Take the next path on

the left hand side and walk down towards the Haybarn Tavern. Just after the tavern, bear right and follow the drive through the park up to the main road. At the road, turn right and continue up the hill towards the Town End side of Troutbeck Village. After a short distance, you reach the Queen's Head Hotel.

PUB - Queen's Head Hotel
see full pub details on page 33

4. From the pub turn left, then left again, up a steep hill, leading to the village. Follow the lane through the village for $1/2$ mile. As you reach a large slate barn on the left hand side of the road, turn left through a metal gate onto a bridle-path, leading to Troutbeck Church at the bottom of the valley. Cross over the next green lane and walk down the hedge-lined track. Go through the gate and cross the field. Leave the field, through the gate next to the beck, and bear left over the slate bridge.

5. Follow the track to the main road with the church on your right. Turn right and walk along the pavement. A short way after the bridge, cross the road and walk up a rocky bridleway at the edge of a wood.

6. Continue past the back of a farm, and after a short distance, leave the track over a stile in the wall on the right hand side. Bear right in the field, following the footpath along the wall. In the second field, bear left slightly, away from the wall on the right, following the yellow marker posts. Cross over the ladder stile, then follow the line of trees on your right. A yellow marker directs you up the hill at a tumbled down wall.

7. Cross over the stile, then turn right onto a walled track. This track eventually brings you back to the Moorhowe Road. Turn left at the road and follow this for around $3/4$ mile back to your car.

FINISH

High Street – A Roman Road

Part of our route goes along High Street, a Roman road built to serve the forts of this northern frontier. It links Galava (Ambleside) with Brovacum (Brougham, near Penrith) and was part of a network of roads connecting forts built between 80 and 90 AD by Agricola. This, at least, is the popular version of local Roman history, but the truth is far from clear.

Much of what we know about Roman place names in the north west is based on three military guide books of the period. Described by historians as 'map-like', they were the RAC route plans of their day. The earliest, the Antonine Itinerary, dates from the early part of the third century AD and lists place names and the distances between them. Applying these names to bumps in the ground is little more than guesswork and identifying places with any confidence can only be done when backed up by archaeological finds with inscriptions – milestones are a good example of this. There have, however, been very few inscriptions found in the area and many known Roman sites have yet to be fully investigated.

So, on your Roman journey from Ambleside to Brougham you can be reasonably confident of heading towards Brovacum - the three itineraries cross-reference to confirm this. But you may have just left Galava, or was it Clanoventa or even Glannibanta. Are you feeling confused, uncertain and kept in the dark? These are feelings you probably share with the average Roman soldier. Just keep on walking – sinister dexter, sinister dexter, sinister dexter.

On this page you will find a variety of useful links that will help you make the most of your time in this stunning part of the world.

Tourist Information

www.touristinformationcentres.com
www.information-britain.co.uk
www.lakes-online.co.uk
www.lakedistrict.gov.uk
www.southlakeland.gov.uk
www.amblesideonline.co.uk
www.broughton-in-furness.co.uk
www.coniston-net.com

Weather

www.meto.gov.uk

Travel

www.nationalrail.co.uk
www.qjump.co.uk
www.thetrainline.com
www.traintaxi.co.uk
www.gobycoach.com
www.travelline.co.uk
www.mountain-goat.com

Equipment

www.gaynors.co.uk
www.millets.co.uk

Walking Groups

www.ramblers.org.uk
www.ralakedistrict.ukf.net

Countryside & Heritage

www.countrysideaccess.gov.uk
www.countryside.gov.uk
www.nationaltrust.org.uk
www.english-nature.org.uk
www.english-heritage.org.uk
www.woodland-trust.org.uk
www.forestry.gov.uk
www.fld.org.uk
www.ospreywatch.co.uk

Beer

www.camra.org.uk

You can also keep up to date on forthcoming publications in this series by going to our website at: www.footstep-publishing.com or www.goodwalkgoodpub.com